THE REP

CW00435306

... .e ..eutre Cambridge
Present

Morning Glory
by Sarah Daniels

23 May - 16 June

First performance
Palace Theatre Watford
20 April 2001

EUROPEAN COMMUNITY

European Regional
Development Fund

Birmingham City Council

WEST
MIDLANDS
ARTS

Providing Theatre for Birmingham

Here at The Rep we are delighted to welcome Jonathan Church as our new Artistic Director. Jonathan joined the company in May from Hampstead Theatre, where he enjoyed great success as Associate Director. Prior to this he was Artistic Director of Salisbury Playhouse. Commenting on his appointment he said:

"Being born and brought up in the Midlands I have been attending shows at Birmingham Rep since an early age and I am delighted to be appointed Artistic Director of a theatre whose work I have followed and much admired over the years.

Andy Allen (Chairman), Jonathan Church and John Stalker.

My involvement with many regional producing theatres has led me to believe that Birmingham Rep can be both a truly local resource, providing the best and most exciting entertainment for the City, the West Midlands and its many communities, and at the same time be a centre of national excellence, creating unique theatre with and for the region that has a significant impact on the rest of the country.."

Jonathan looks forward to meeting and talking to members of our audience soon!

Artistic Director
Jonathan Church

Chief Executive
John Stalker

Associate Artistic Director
Anthony Clark

Birmingham Repertory Theatre
Broad Street, Birmingham B1 2EP

Administration 0121 245 2000
Facsimile 0121 245 2100
Box Office 0121 236 4455
Minicom 0121 245 2025
www.birmingham-rep.co.uk

Morning Glory
by Sarah Daniels

Production Credits

Multimedia Replications Ltd – Experts in CD, floppy copying & hardware

Guinness, Park Royal Brewery, London

Masquerade Fancy Dress & Theatrical Hire

Booker Cash and Carry, Watford

Shopmobility, Watford

CD Warehouse

British Red Cross Society

Medal News supplied by Token Publishing

Sony Centre, Watford

Multi media replications

Tate & Lyle

Pains Wessex safety systems

Liz and Ben Stone, Bristol

Mr Kipling, exceedingly good cakes

Manor Bakeries, Windsor

The Watford Observer

Garrods Ltd, Kings Langley

Newport Lighter fluid

Dixons, Watford

Adele
Brigit Forsyth

Rose
Ann Rye

Grace
Charmian May

Melissa
Siren Turkesh

Luke
Louis Tamone

Brett
Scott Neal

Director
Lawrence Till

Assistant Director
Deborah Sathe

Designer
Patrick Connellan

Lighting Designer
Symon Harner

Sound
Gina Hills

Deputy Stage Manager
Vicki Morrison

Biographies

Sarah Daniels
Writer

Sarah Daniels lives in London. Her first play, Ripen Our Darkness, was produced at the Royal Court Theatre Upstairs in 1981. The following year, Neaptide won the George Devine Award and opened in the Cottesloe at the Royal National Theatre in 1986. Her 1983 play, Masterpieces, premiered at the Royal Exchange Manchester and the Royal Court Theatre Downstairs, winning Sarah the Most Promising Playwright Award from both London Theatre Critics and Drama Magazine. It has subsequently been produced around the world and in 1999 was selected by the National Theatre as one of the plays of the century.

Sarah's other plays include The Devil's Gateway (Royal Court Theatre Upstairs, 1983); Bythrite (Royal Court Theatre 1986); The Gut Girls (Albany Empire, 1988); Beside Herself (Royal Court Theatre Downstairs, 1990); Head-Rot Holiday (Clean Break Theatre 1993); The Madness Of Esme and Shaz (Royal Court Theatre Upstairs 1994); Blow your House Down (Live Theatre Co, Newcastle, 1995); Taking Breath (BT. Connections, National Theatre, 1999); Best Mates (Royal National Theatre, Educational Department tour 2000).

Sarah has also written for television including Eastenders and, for the past fifteen years, Grange Hill. As well as her original plays for radio she has also written for Westway, the medical soap for the World Service.

Adele
Brigit Forsyth

Brigit trained at The Royal Academy of Dramatic Art where she won the Emile Littler Award. Theatre includes: Single Spies (West Yorkshire Playhouse); Lady Bracknell in The Importance of Being Earnest (The Royal Exchange Manchester); Amanda Wingfield in The Glass Menagerie (Theatr Clwyd); Viv in Tom and Viv (The Library Manchester); Annie in The Norman Conquests (The Globe and Apollo Theatres, London); Dusa in Dusa, Stas, Fish and Vi (Hampstead and The Mayfair, London). Other work includes: Little Murders and The Comedy of Errors (The Royal Exchange, Manchester);The Price (Library, Manchester); Effie's Burning by Valerie Windsor (Library Theatre Manchester & National Theatre) and several international tours for Derek Nimmo including The Maintenance Man and You Must Be The Husband. Television: Brigit is probably best known as Thelma from Whatever Happened to the Likely Lads for the BBC. Her extensive television work covers two series of Tom, Dick and Harriet for Thames, two series of The Practice for Granada, two series of Sharon and Elsie for the BBC and many other dramas and comedies including: Nice Town, Dangerfield, Bazaar and Rummage, Murder Most Horrid, Casualty, The Dark Season and The Master of Ballantrae for the BBC, Wycliffe for HTV, The Ward, The Sinners and Adam Smith for Granada, Running Wild and Poirot for LWT and Boon for Central. She has recently played Francine Pratt in four series of Playing The Field for Tiger Aspect. She has also played Thelma in a feature film of Whatever Happened to the Likely Lads for EMI and appeared in the Channel 4 film Stanley's Vision with Ben Kingsley.
Brigit also appears in the film Fanny & Elvis by Kay Mellor. In addition to all this Brigit has worked extensively in radio.

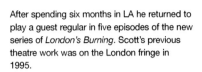

Grace
Charmian May

Charmian trained at the
Royal Academy of
Dramatic Art. Recent theatre includes: *Semi
Detached, The Man Who Came to Dinner* and
A String of Pearls (all at the Chichester Festival
Theatre); *Move Over Mrs Markham* (Middle
East and Far East Tour). West End credits
include: *Under the Greenwood Tree* (Vaudeville
Theatre) which was adapted and produced by
Patrick Garland; *84 Charing Cross Road*
(Ambassadors Theatre); *Look No Hans!* (Strand
Theatre). Recent television includes: *Kavanagh
QC, The Worst Witch, Midsomer Murders,
Family Affairs, The Bill, Keeping Up
Appearances, the Upper Hand, The Darling
Buds of May, Love Hurts, The Politician's Wife,
Soldier Soldier, Pie in the Sky* and *Touching
Evil*. Film includes: *Bridget Jones' Diary,
Highlander IV, Demon in my View, Paper Mask,
A Fish Called Wanda* and *Britannia Hospital*.
Charmian has written a one-woman show,
Celebrating Shakespeare, which she has
performed in theatres, schools and colleges
around the UK and in Boston, Chicago and
New York.

Brett
Scott Neal

Scott trained at The Anna
Scher Theatre between
1989 – 1996. His first
acting roles were in
EastEnders, Bramwell and
The Bill. Scott's first big break came when he
landed one of the lead roles in the highly
successful film *Beautiful Thing*. He then went
on to play the lead in the independent film *The
Wonderland Experience*. Shortly after the
filming in India he was cast as PC Luke Ashton
in *The Bill* which he played for two years.

After spending six months in LA he returned to
play a guest regular in five episodes of the new
series of *London's Burning*. Scott's previous
theatre work was on the London fringe in
1995.

Rose
Ann Rye

Ann trained at Morley
College at the Webber
Douglas. Her theatre work
spans the National Theatre,
The Royal Court and the
West End and theatres all over the country.
Ann has appeared in many TV dramas and
soaps from *St Joan* and *A Farwell to Arms* to
the original *Dr Finlay's Casebook*. Recent
theatre includes: *The Beauty Queen of
Lenane* (The Library Theatre, Manchester);
The Life and Death of a Buffalo Soldier and
The Beaux Stratagem (Bristol Old Vic); *A
Cream Cracker Under the Settee*, The first
stage version of Alan Bennett's *Talking Heads*
directed by Lawrence Till (Octagon Bolton);
the first production of *Mr Wonderful* (Derby
Playhouse). Film includes: *Don't look Now, In
this house of Brede, Wide Eyed & Legless*
and the recent *Blow Dry*. Ann was a member
of the Stables Theatre Company (Granada's
unique joint TV/Theatre venture) and wrote
and presented her own slot on ATV's *Women
Today*. She has done extensive work for
radio, including short stories, drama,
documentaries, religious programmes and
Women's Hour. Recent TV includes:
*Heartbeat, Casualty, Always & Everyone, Big
Meg, Little Meg* and *Wilmot*. She was
recently seen as Emiline Pendry in
Coronation Street.

Biographies

Luke
Louis Tamone

Louis trained at Redroofs Theatre School and then Arts Educational where he appeared as Danny in *Grease,* Frederick in *A Little Night Music* and Herman in *Sweet Charity* amongst others. He has done extensive voiceovers for Oxford University Press and film dubbing for Paramount and Tristar including *The City of Lost Children.* Television includes: *Pie in the Sky, Top of the Pops* and *The Steve Wright Show.*

Melissa
Siren Turkesh

Siren has recently graduated from the BA Acting course at Italia Conti. Theatre whilst training includes: Rose in *Byrthrite,* Mona (then) in *Come Back to The Five and Dime, Jimmy Dean Jimmy Dean* and Baptiste in *The Music Lovers.* Professional theatre includes: Yonah in *Children of Eden* (Lando Theatre) and Mary Magdalene in a musical comedy *Roll over Jehovah* (the New End Hampstead).

Lawrence Till
Director

Lawrence is the Artistic Director of the Palace Theatre, Watford and previously Artistic Director of the Octagon Theatre, Bolton. He has been nominated three times as Best Director in the Barclays British Regional Theatre Awards organised by the Theatrical Management Association. For the Palace Theatre Lawrence has directed *Talking Heads, Blithe Spirit, Cor, Blimey!* and *Martha, Josie and the Chinese Elvis.* His production of *Translations* by Brian Friel was nominated for the Barclays Best Touring Production Award in 2000. Lawrence has directed over fifty productions including premieres by Paul Abbott (*Binnin' It, Possession*), Alan Bennett (*Bed Among the Lentils*), Henry Livings (*The Rough Side of the Boards*), Bill Naughton (*Derby Day, Annie & Fanny from Bolton to Rome*), Dominic McHale (*The Resurrectionists*) and Charlotte Jones (*Martha, Josie and the Chinese Elvis*). Second productions include plays by Jim Cartwright (*Little Voice*), Christina Reid (*Joyriders*) and Philip Ridley (*The Pitchfork Disney, The Fastest Clock in the Universe, Ghost from a Perfect Place*). In 1998 he was invited by the British Council and the National Theatre of Turkey to direct Peter Shaffer's *Black Comedy* in Istanbul.

Deborah Sathe
Assistant Director

Deborah is currently on an Arts Council
Trainee Director Bursary at the Palace
Theatre, Watford. Deborah trained at the
Royal Academy of Music, and gained a
drama degree at Birmingham University. On
leaving university she directed *Into the
Woods* at the Edinburgh Festival for Plunge!
Productions. She recently left the Leicester
Haymarket Theatre where she was the Youth
Theatre Leader and Natak Project
Co-ordinator. She directed many productions
including: *Beyond the Land of Hattamala,
The Eighth Key, Far Away Tales, Children of
the Blitz, The Fairy Tale that has Never Been
Told*. She also wrote and directed plays for
Aurat (Asian women's project). Whilst at the
Haymarket she directed the London premiere
of *Honk!* at the Landor Theatre. At the Palace
Theatre, Watford Deborah has been Assistant
Director on *A Taste of Honey, Aladdin and his
Wonderful Lamp* and *Martha, Josie and the
Chinese Elvis*.

Patrick Connelan
Designer

Patrick won the Linbury Prize for stage
design in 1987 and has worked in the West
End and regional theatre.
His most recent theatre credits include:
Perfect Days (Wolsey Theatre, Ipswich and
Greenwich); *Leader of the Pack* (No 1 tour);
A View from the Bridge (Harrogate Theatre);
The Silent Witch (RNT Springboard and
Birmingham Repertory Theatre), *St Joan*
(Birmingham Repertory Theatre) and *My
Best Friend* (Birmingham Repertory
Theatre/Hampstead Theatre co-production);
The Blue Room (Bolton Octagon); *A
Passionate Woman* (Gloria Theatre, Athens);
A Midsummer Night's Dream and *She
Knows You Know* (New Vic Theatre); *Big
Nose* (Belgrade Theatre/set design); *Phil And
Jill And Jill And Phil* (Swan Theatre
Worcester and Belgrade Coventry) and the
set design For *The Wizard of Oz* (Leicester
Haymarket). Other credits include: *A
Passionate Woman* (Comedy Theatre);
Misery (Criterion Theatre); *Pygmalion, Cider
With Rosie, The Pied Piper*, and *Julius
Caesar* (Birmingham Repertory Theatre);
*Leader of the Pack, Neville's Island, The
Wedding and Limestone Cowboy* (Belgrade
Theatre Coventry); *Salad Days* (Vaudeville
Theatre); *Conduct Unbecoming* (National
Tour); *Misery* (Leicester Haymarket);
Macbeth and *Twelfth Night* (Mercury Theatre
Colchester); *Time And The Conways* (Bolton
Octagon); *Top Girls* (Salisbury Playhouse
And The Drum Plymouth). Future
productions include: *The Dice House*
(Coventry Belgrade).

Biographies

Symon Harner
Lighting Designer.

Lighting designs for Birmingham Repertory Theatre Company include: *Belonging*, *The Slight Witch*, *My Dad's Corner Shop*, *My Best Friend*, *Perpetua*, *Trips*, *Transmissions 1998*, *The Tenant Of Wildfell Hall*, *A Shaft of Sunlight* (a co-production with Tamasha Theatre Company, also at Battersea Arts Centre), *East Lynne*, *The New Menoza*, *Playing By The Rules* (also at The Drill Hall, London), *The Magic Toyshop*, *Kafka's Dick* (and National Tour), *The Turn Of The Screw*, *Metamorphosis* (and National Tour), *The Threepenny Opera*, Tony Harrison's *"V"*, *Pinocchio*, *The Canal Ghost*. Other designs include: *Silence*, *The Hired Man* and *Tales From The Vienna Woods* (Theatre Royal, Plymouth) the National Tour of *Inamorata's Pigtales* which opened at Bristol Old Vic, *The Trial* for The Mouse People.

Carole Todd
Choreographer

Carole recently worked at the Palace Theatre, Watford as choreographer on *Martha, Josie and the Chinese Elvis*. As Director, Carole's many credits include: *Elvis the Musical* and *Ferry Cross the Mersey* in the West End, UK, Australia and Canada as well as three productions of *A Slice of Saturday Night*, two of *Blues in the Night*, *Stand by Me*, *Lanza the Last Seranade*, *Chicago*, *Grease*, *Doctor Who*, *James and the Giant Peach*, *Wizard of Oz*, *Cowardy Custard*, *The Rivals*, *Dancing in the Street* and recent concerts for Elaine Page, Jane McDonald and Gary Wilmot.
In contrast, recent tours of *Girls' Night Out* and *Girls Night Out in Ibiza* (about Male Strippers), *Strippers* (about female strippers) and *The Fly* (with no strippers at all!). Many Television series and specials include: *Lenny Beige* (Channel 4), Stravinsky's *Renard The Fox* (Channel 4), *Morecombe and Wise* (Thames) *Oh Boy* two series (not the original!) and *Benny Hill* (Thames). Film Choreography includes: *Morons from Outer Space*, *Prick up your Ears*, *Treasure Island*, *A Night on the Town* and *Julie and the Cadillacs*.
Choreography includes: *Return to the Forbidden Planet*, *Jack to a King*, *Tribute to the Blues Brothers*, *La Cenerentola* at the Royal Opera House, *Wild Oats* at the National Theatre, many productions of *The Mikado* in the UK, Los Angeles and Australia. Last year, she directed and staged *Lanza, the Last Serenade* and *Stand by Me*, a motown based musical, *Music to watch Girls by* with Gary Wilmot, Mike Holoway's *Rock n Roll Rollercoaster Show*, *Me and My Girl*, *The Mikado* for Opera Queensland in Brisbane and Lily Savage in *Snow White* (Southampton).

_{THE}REP

Birmingham Repertory Theatre

Birmingham Repertory Theatre is one of Britain's leading national theatre companies. From its base in the city centre, The Rep produces over twenty new productions each year, many of which transfer to London and also tour nationally and internationally. In the last 24 months nine of our productions have been seen in London including *Two Pianos, Four Hands, Baby Doll, My Best Friend, Terracotta, The Gift, The Snowman, A Wedding Story* and most recently *The Ramayana*. Our productions of *Hamlet and Twelfth Night* also enjoyed a successful major tour last year.

In October 1999 The Rep completed a £7.5 million refurbishment which has transformed the theatre, renewed vital stage equipment, increased access and improved public areas.

The commissioning and production of new work lies at the core of The Rep's programme. In 1998 the company launched The Door, a venue dedicated to the production and presentation of new work. This, together with an investment of almost £1 million over four years in commissioning new drama from some of Britain's brightest and best writing talent, gives The Rep a unique position in British theatre. Indeed, through the extensive commissioning of new work The Rep is providing vital opportunities for the young and emerging writing talent that will lead the way in the theatre of the future. This season *Morning Glory* was joined by new works from Nigel Moffatt (*Musical Youth*) and Jonathan Harvey (*Out in the Open*).

Up Next...

Hotting up for the summer in style, a week of dance from *Nederlands Dans Theater 2* (29 - 30 May), and *CandoCo* (1 - 2 June) is followed by the colourful and passionate musical *Blues in the Night* (8 - 30 June). In The Door, the annual Transmissions Festival is taking place from 4 - 14 July, giving our young writers a chance to see their completed scripts performed by professional actors. This is followed by *The Wedding*, a new translation of *Respectable Wedding* by Brecht, performed by the Young Rep Senior Group from 19 - 21 July.

For more information about any of these productions call our Sales Team on 0121 236 4455 or visit www.birmingham-rep.co.uk.

We look forward to welcoming you to The Rep again soon!

Palace Theatre Watford

The Palace Theatre is a beautiful Edwardian theatre restored to its original splendour and is the only repertory theatre in Hertfordshire and one of the leading producers of theatre in East England. We present a varied annual programme of productions and one pantomime to a local and London-based audience of over 100,000 people a year. Many of our productions go on to tour nationally or transfer into the West End and are renowned for their quality, success and diversity including drama, adaptations, new plays and comedies. These productions attract first class artists – actors, writers, directors and designers – who regularly win critical acclaim.

Our commitment to new and exciting work is well documented. World premieres from previous seasons include *Elton John's Glasses* by David Farr which won the Writer's Guild Award for Best Regional Play in 1997, the stage version of *The Talented Mr Ripley* by Phyllis Nagy, Simon Gray's *The Late Middle Classes*, directed by Harold Pinter was awarded the 1999 TMA award for Best New Play and most recently we presented *Martha, Josie and the Chinese Elvis* a new comedy by Charlotte Jones in February 2001.

The Palace Theatre is a well-established flagship for artistic, educational and cultural provision and a focus for arts and creativity for the people of Watford, Hertfordshire and beyond. Our mission is to recognise the quality of that past and embrace the opportunities of the future in order to create and co-produce plays which will excite, delight and inspire our wide-ranging audience.

This mission will be aided by the Arts Council of England's Lottery Funded refurbishment planned for 2002.
This will help us to shape the Palace Theatre's future even more successfully.

We have a history of successful co-productions with regional theatres and commercial producers, enabling our shows to be seen nationally and in the West End. The Palace Theatre Watford is delighted to be collaborating with Birmingham Repertory Theatre and the Cambridge Arts Theatre on this production of *Morning Glory*.

Artistic Director
Lawrence Till
Administrative Director
Mary Caws
Office & Casting Co-ordinator
Andrea Bath
Director of Development
Jane Steele
Marketing Manager
Craig Titley
Production Manager
Deborah Sawyerr
Finance Manager
Harry Holt ACMA

(01923 235455)
Palace Theatre Watford is a registered charity number 1056950

Cambridge Arts Theatre

Cambridge Arts Theatre
Cambridge Arts Theatre
6 St Edward's Passage,
Cambridge, CB2 3PJ

Patron: Her Majesty Queen Elizabeth,
The Queen Mother
Founder: Lord Keynes
Executive Director: Ian Ross
PA to the Executive Director:
Sally Marsh

Cambridge Arts Theatre was founded in 1936
by the economist, John Maynard Keynes,
and is one of the most famous and well-
loved homes of drama, dance, opera and
comedy in Britain. Following a multi-million
pound refurbishment, it continues to stage a
wide variety of entertainment and, through an
active education and community programme,
to develop high quality live performance
which is enriching, enjoyable and accessible.

Head of Operations - Raymond Cross
Technical Stage Manager - Nick Stewart
Deputy Stage Manager - Andy Stubbs
Chief Electrician - Alistair Boitz
Deputy Chief Electrician - Paul Siequien
Building Maintenance - Paul Huggins
Apprentice Technician - Sam McLeod
Senior Stage Door Keeper - Andy Sealy
Stage Door Keepers
Nigel Draper, David Etchells

Finance Manager - Lisa Winter
Finance Assistant - Connie Weston

Marketing Manager - Nicola Upson
Marketing and Press Officer -
Dawn Flack
Marketing Assistant - Polly Griffiths

Graphic Designer - Nicky Hupe

Education & Community Manager -
Roberta Hamond
Education Officer - Heather Lilley

Corporate Manager - Sally Marsh

Front of House Manager -
Matthew Human

Box Office Manager - Vivien Mayne
Deputy Box Office Manager -
Tracey Stone
Box Office Supervisor - Emma Nicol

Corporate Members

3i plc; Albera Networks; Anglo-American
Association Ltd; ARM; Arthur Andersen;
Bidwells; Bland, Brown & Cole; Cambridge
Building Society; Davis Langdon & Everest;
Deloitte & Touche; Edward Thackray Building
Ltd; Eversheds; Hannah Reed Associates;
Heffers; Local Examinations Syndicate,
Cambridge; Lorimer Longhurst & Lees; ntl:
Cambridge Ltd; N W Brown Group Ltd;
Peters Elworthy & Moore; Ridgeons Ltd;
Roxboro Group; Scientific Generics;
Tattersalls Ltd; Taylor Vinters; The Marshall
Motor Group; The Royal Society of
Chemistry; The Technology Partnership; TTP
Communications Ltd; Virco UK Ltd; Wates
Construction; Westley & Huff.

Cambridge Arts Theatre gratefully
acknowledges financial assistance from:

eastengland|arts

Cambridge Arts Theatre is managed by The
Cambridge Arts Theatre Trust Ltd, registered
in England No. 03536370, registered charity
No. 1075727. Registered office as above. VAT
Registration Number 213 267784.

Developing young local talent

The Transmissions Scheme

In July 2000, The Door played host to eighteen new plays by local writers aged between 12 and 25. A company of ten professional actors, directors, a designer and technical and production staff brought these scripts to life culminating in a hugely successful public festival. The festival was made possible by the dedication and creative talent of these writers who had met regularly over six months on Saturday afternoons in the theatre.

Young writers from Moseley to Staffordshire developed their scripts in workshops led by established playwrights Carl Miller, Noel Greig and Maya Chowdhry. Not only did they get the opportunity to learn the craft of playwriting but also they developed their critical skills when each other's plays were shared amongst the group! The generosity of the writers towards each other was positive and interactive, leading to a truly collaborative festival.

In February 2000 six actors came into the theatre for a week to try out the scripts which were in a 'state of development'. As the actors and directors demonstrated to the writers what worked on the stage, they went back to write another draft! By May 2000 the completed drafts were tentatively handed over to the theatre.

Each and every writer had completed a script and the impossible task of programming eighteen plays into two weeks with four public performances began. Meetings between staff at The Rep, directors and the design team began and the puzzle of making this a reality slowly began to be solved. A

flexible stage was designed allowing one play to flow easily into another – not an easy task when eight plays were to be staged on the first Saturday. Then the task of asking ten professional actors to play over a hundred parts between them began.

Each and every space within the theatre was turned into a rehearsal room and the writers poured backstage to offer their advice on character development. The first night arrived and The Door was full of fellow writers, friends, family and the general public gathering to witness this exciting event. The energy both off stage and on filled the auditorium with the young writers taking their well-deserved bow at the end of the evening.

If that wasn't enough we started the process all over again in November with a new group of writers, who have just met the actors and directors for the first time in a week of workshops on the first three scenes of their plays. Early signs are that the range and quality of the work will be as outstanding as last year. Look out for the fruits of their labours in the Transmissions 2001 Festival from 4 – 14 July.

Young Rep

The Rep's Youth Theatre

Following the successes of the past year, the senior group of The Young Rep returns to The Door with a new production of *The Wedding* by Bertolt Brecht from 19 - 21 July.

The guests are arriving and Dad's already hitting the bottle, the bride has a guilty secret and the groom has made all his own furniture. Written when he was in early twenties, this one act play by one of the 20th century's greatest dramatists combines satire and slapstick to depict one happy day where nearly everything goes wrong ...

Tickets: £4.50, £3.50 (concessions)

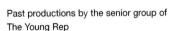

Past productions by the senior group of The Young Rep

For more information about Transmissions and The Young Rep contact the Education Department on 0121 245 2093.
To book your tickets for Transmissions Festival 2001 and
The Wedding call our Sales Team on 0121 236 4455

Sarah Daniels
Morning Glory

based on an idea by
Teddy Kiendl

faber and faber

First published in 2001
by Faber and Faber Limited
3 Queen Square, London WC1N 3AU
First published in the United States in 2001 by Faber and Faber Inc.
an affiliate of Farrar, Straus and Giroux LLC, New York

Typeset by Country Setting, Kingsdown, Kent CT14 8ES
Printed in England by Intype London Ltd

A CIP record for this book
is available from the British Library

ISBN 0–571–21211–5

2 4 6 8 10 9 7 5 3 1

With thanks to Teddy Kiendl
for all his dramaturgical advice.
Without Teddy this play
would not have been written

With love and thanks to Lawrence Till
S.D.

Characters

Rose
Grace
Adele

Brett
Melissa
Luke

Part One

SCENE ONE

Adele, wearing a simple grey skirt, blouse and large crucifix, is standing by a hospital bed. The occupant of the bed is unseen, but the constant bleep, bleep, bleep of the life-support machine can be heard underneath Adele's confession. Her left hand is cut and has a handkerchief tied around it to staunch the blood.

Adele (*to the occupant of the bed*) I didn't mean it to come to this. I can't believe it. I am so, so sorry. I was trying, if you only knew how much, to make amends. But it's all gone so terribly wrong. I shouldn't be here. But I can't go. I saw a magpie on the way here – and I have to stay until I see another one. It was my father's fault. I can remember sitting on his knee in a park. I couldn't have been five years old. We'd seen one but he said we couldn't go home until we'd seen another. I was cold and shivering so I said, 'There Daddy. Look, there's another one.' And somehow he was persuaded, even though he hadn't seen it, that it counted because I had, and we were able to go home, but I was never able to tell him I made it up. I'm so sorry. I'm so sorry. Are you aware of anything, can you hear me, or are you just waiting to be switched off?

(*then to God*) God please help me, please. I'll do anything if . . . I'll tell you everything, Holy Father, if you'll make it somehow come right. Please hear my prayer. I know I've done wrong but that wasn't ever my intention – quite the opposite. If only I'd not gone to that memorial service. But when I saw the notice in the paper, well it seemed like a God-sent opportunity. Yes, it did, God. I'd been looking for her for years.

She didn't recognise me at first, then, when she did, she was rather put out and that's putting it very mildly, but luckily for me – or so I thought at the time – she was very agitated about why her old colleague Rose had not turned up. So when I offered to give her a lift to Watford to find out what had happened to Rose she was hardly in a position to refuse. No mean feat from Southwark Cathedral to Watford and an education. I'd always thought that there couldn't be anything worse than driving on the London Orbital but getting on to the ring road here seemed like a kamikaze feat requiring reckless bravery of gladiatorial proportions. Not that I cared a bit. I was pleased, absolutely delighted to be doing Grace Leighton, CBE, a good turn. You see *then* I thought that just giving her a lift would put me back in favour and I could go back to my life knowing that I'd been forgiven. I can also remember that I thought there could well be a hundred and one reasons why Rose wasn't at the service and that Grace's agitation was an old worrier's over-reaction. But I was wrong about that as well.

SCENE TWO

Rose's living room. It has been ransacked. The telephone lead has been cut in half. The radio is on. (The kids have changed the station from Radio Four to Capital Gold.) Rose is unconscious. Grace turns the radio off and then kneels next to Rose and rubs her hand.

Grace Rose, it's Grace. Can you hear me? (*Puts her handbag and Order of Service down and tries to feel for a pulse.*) Rose? I've come from Barty's memorial service in London to find you. When you didn't turn up, I knew something must have happened. I tried ringing but I can see now why I didn't get an answer. Whoever it was has cut the telephone wires. But we're here now and you're

going to be just fine. It's me. Rose, please wake up now.
You need to wake up. You feel so cold. Please just try
and hold on.

*Adele minus the bandage on her hand and not dressed
as a nun comes in clutching her handbag and a packet
of cigarettes.*

Grace (*opening her handbag*) What kept you?

Adele Public phone boxes.

Grace But you did get through? (*She takes a compact
mirror from her own handbag.*)

Adele Yes, but because the phone boxes were out of
order I had to ask the newsagent to call the ambulance
and I didn't like to just stand there while he was phoning
so I thought I'd better buy something.

Grace (*holds the mirror to Rose's mouth*) No matter.
Just see if you can find some blankets. (*She looks at the
mirror but it doesn't tell her anything.*)

Adele Is she . . .? Err . . . breathing?

Grace Quick as you can. (*Snaps the compact shut,
returns it to her bag.*)

Adele Do you think it wise to go rifling through,
touching things before the police get here?

*Grace gives her a look and Adele casts her eye around
the room for blankets.*

Grace Try the bedroom. (*to Rose*) What has happened?
Who's done this to you? Rose, it's me. Grace.

Adele (*coming back into the room with a duvet*) You
should see the state of it in there. It looks like they've
been through her wardrobe, trying on her shoes.

Grace Help me put her in the recovery position and then
we'll put that over her.

9

Adele I don't think we should touch her, do you? I mean they say not to move –

Grace I will take full responsibility. Just give me a hand –

Adele (*helps Grace*) If she chokes on her own vomit, on your head be it.

> *They roll Rose on her side and put the duvet around Rose. In the process Grace's handbag gets placed at the end of it.*

Grace (*feels Rose tap her hand*) Rose? (*to Adele*) Did you see that? Her hand moved.

Adele I can't say that I –

Grace Rose? Can you do that again? Are you conscious? Can you hear me? Do you know who I am?

Adele Don't you think that perhaps we should try and get in touch with someone, a relative or something?

Grace She did. She moved.

Adele I think we could probably all do with a nice hot sugary drink. Strong tea might do the trick.

> *Rose taps Grace's hand again.*

Grace There. Yes. Wonderful. How are you feeling?

> *Rose continues to tap, Grace tries to work it out.*

Dash dot dash dot – C. Dash dash dash – O. Dot dash dot – R – Corn? No, Rose you've not landed in a field. There isn't any corn. you are in your own home. (*Rose taps again. Dash dot dot dot. Dot dash. Dash dash dot.*) B-A-G. Bag? What bag? Come again? Rose? I don't understand.

Adele I think she must mean your handbag.

Grace My handbag? What's that got to do with anything?

Adele (*removing her bag*) It's on her foot.

Grace (*realising*) Pressing on her corns.

Adele More than likely. In my book corns are the curse for the post-menopausal.

Grace (*lets go of Rose's hand to tuck the duvet around her. To Rose*) You always were cursed with them as I remember. I'm so sorry, I didn't realise. For one awful moment I thought that we'd lost you. (*Takes Rose's hand again.*) It won't be much longer now, the ambulance is on its way. (*then no response*) Rose? Rose?

Adele Perhaps a large brandy?

Grace (*but Rose's hand is limp. To Adele*) Have you got a biro? Or something of that nature?

    Adele looks at her.

Preferably now, not next week.

Adele (*opens her handbag and tips out the contents including an old-fashioned Dunhill lighter and a small bottle of lavender oil*) You might be better off with smelling salts – only of course no one has them these days, or –

    Grace gives her a look and Adele picks up the biro and gives it to her.

Grace Don't slip back. Rose, stay with me. (*Starts tapping in morse code with the pen on the floor by Rose's head.*)

Adele – any idea where to get them. (*Picks up lavender oil, takes the top off and waves it under Rose's nose.*) Trouble is this smells too nice. I know. (*She starts to pull a loose feather from the duvet.*)

Grace Just hold on, stay awake. Tom Boy. (*Dash. Dash, dash, dash. Dash, dash. Dash, dot, dot, dot. Dash, dash,*

dash. Dash, dot, dash, dash.) Tom Boy. This is Mad Lad. (*Dash, dash. Dot, dash. Dash dot, dot. Dot, dash, dot, dot. Dot, dash. Dash, dot, dot.*)

Adele (*over Grace's tapping. Plucks a feather and holds it up*) Eureka. (*She proceeds to try and set light to it with her lighter.*) The pong from this will bring her round if anything can –

Grace Over. Do you copy? Please, please, Rose, respond. It's very important. This is Grace. Code-name Mad Lad.

Adele (*unable to light the feather. Looks for a label on the duvet*) I might have guessed – it's been fire-proofed.

Grace Please come back. Don't you dare just fade away. Not now. Rose, I need you here – with me. Please.

The sound of ambulance sirens can be heard.

Adele It's here. (*She collects her bag, and goes to the door.*) Here it is.

Grace I'll go with her. You stay here.

Adele Here?

Grace Wait for the police and when they've gone make sure you clear up every inch of this mess.

Adele looks at her open-mouthed, but before she can say anything –

Then wait for me to get in touch.

SCENE THREE

Brett's flat. A carrier bag containing Rose's old tin cash-box. Luke and Melissa are dancing to Madonna's 'Lucky Star'. Melissa looks at Luke and they start to dance to a worked-out routine. Brett comes in from another room, sending a text message on his mobile phone.

Brett Please, no, don't. Don't do this to me.

Melissa What?

Brett You should never have been allowed to watch television on a Sunday morning.

Luke But learning to dance like Pan's People is what me and Mel live for.

Brett But you're crap.

Melissa Then we've got it right.

Brett But nobody knows that. Nobody even remembers who they were.

Luke They do if they watch TV on Sunday mornings.

Melissa Everyone knows who they were. They were on *Top of the Pops* for years.

Brett Yeah? Well, they never danced to Madonna. They were grannies by the time this came out.

He stops the music, fast-forwarding to 'Like a Virgin', and he and Luke go into their 'Reservoir Dogs' routine.

'It's not about a nice girl who meets a sensitive boy. Now granted that's what "True Blue" is about, no argument about that.'

Melissa What?

13

Brett You don't remember 'True Blue'? That was a big ass hit for Madonna. Shit, I don't even follow this *Top of the Pops* shit and I've at least heard of 'True Blue'.

Melissa What are you talking like that for?

Brett (*to Luke*) 'Where was I?'

Luke You said, '"True Blue" was about a nice girl who finds a sensitive fella. But "Like a Virgin" was a metaphor for big dicks.'

Brett Reckon it could be a metaphor for me and Melissa, Mr Pink?

Melissa Oh, I get it.

Brett Do you? But when it comes to me you'll be like a virgin. Won't you for me?

He grabs her and starts to dance with her by grinding his crotch into hers. He then tries to kiss her on the mouth. She struggles and pulls away. As she does so she trips over the carrier bag containing the tin cash-box, and there is a sound of glass smashing.

Luke Now look what you've done.

Melissa Me? That's right. Not.

Brett (*kicks the bag into the corner of the room*) Useless garbage. I told you we should've chucked it in the cut.

Luke We don't even know what's in it.

Brett It's not folding money, is it? Just leave it.

Melissa (*sensing Brett's mood, turns the music up again*) Okay, okay. Let's get back to the party.

They start to dance again.

Luke Shotgun?

Brett Yeah, and the first one to make a mess has to strip to music.

Luke That's right.

Melissa I don't remember agreeing to this.

Brett The only thing you need to remember is Paige.

Melissa What about her?

Luke She messed up big time.

Brett (*finds an old rusty screwdriver and punches a hole in each can. Then as a toast*) May she rest in peace.

They nod in agreement and each of them picks up a can. Holding a finger over the hole, they hold the cans up to their mouths and release the ring pull and their fingers over the hole, causing the whole contents of the can to tip down their throats. Brett's mobile phone rings. He answers it and spills some.

Brett (*to phone*) Yes? Twenty minutes. Fifty quid.

Luke What you going to take off?

Brett Yeah. (*He goes to get his coat.*)

Melissa You're not supposed to put more clothes on.

Luke Yeah, you spilled some. Start stripping Brett.

Brett I can't get into this right now.

Melissa Yeah, like I could have got away with saying that. Not.

Brett I've got to go out.

Melissa But –

Brett You got a problem with that?

Melissa No.

Brett Good.

Brett goes. Luke opens another lager and offers Melissa one.

Melissa What is the matter with him?

Luke Nothing.

Melissa Where's he keep going to?

Luke Dunno.

Melissa I thought you were his best mate.

Luke What you don't know you can't tell anyone.

Melissa Okay, so you don't know, but if you had to guess what would you think it was?

Luke (*shrugs*) Drugs.

Melissa (*shocked*) Drugs?? Drugs?! He's dealing drugs? Excuse me? (*outraged*) How come he's never offered us any?

Luke Dunno. I only said maybe. Maybe he's not. I dunno.

The CD plays like a prayer.

Melissa Let's not waste time while he's gone. C'mon, you know it's your favourite.

Luke You go ahead if you want. I'm not in the mood.

Melissa (*strokes his face*) Luke –

Luke Get off.

Rose's flat. Grace comes in, carrying an overnight case and pushing Rose, who's in a wheelchair. Adele greets them.

Adele Welcome home, Rose. Let me take that. (*Takes the overnight case and extends her other hand to Rose.*) Pleased to meet you, I'm –

Grace Is the tea ready?

Adele In a jiffy. (*She goes.*)

Rose Who the bloody hell is she?

Grace Just someone –

Rose I thought I'd made it clear when you visited me in hospital that I didn't want your money.

Grace It's not costing a brass farthing.

Rose I don't want any charity either. Not from you and certainly not from a complete stranger.

Grace It's not charity. It's what she owes us.

Rose She can't owe me anything. I've never clapped eyes on her before. I don't even know her name. You never even warned me –

Grace I'd rather hoped you'd be pleased. This room was not a pretty sight. Can you remember what –

Rose You asked her to clear it up?

Grace Her name's Adele. Now, don't let's embarrass her. We can talk about it later.

Adele comes back into the room with a tray of tea.

Rose Adele, what are you doing here?

Adele Just helping out.

Rose But why?

Adele Grace asked me to.

Rose Is she paying you?

Adele No, no.

Grace Satisfied? (*Picks up paper.*) Now let's just settle down and have a look to see where *Songs of Praise* is coming from this evening.

Rose Heaven preserve us. (*to Adele*) What is it you're supposed to owe me?

Grace For goodness sake, Rose. Sugar, Adele?

Adele Sugar? Oh yes. Sugar, Mister Speaker, now who dares to laugh at sugar, eh? I'll just get it. (*She goes.*)

Rose Is she the full shilling?

Grace Bit doddery, but otherwise completely compos mentis. It's you.

Rose Me?

Grace Your interrogation. It's unnerving her.

Adele comes back with the sugar.

Adele I really am very sorry about what's happened.

Rose Thank you, but I don't want you to be doing this out of pity.

Adele No, of course not. It's Grace and you who are doing me a favour.

Rose I'm sorry I'm not making head nor tail of this.

Grace Milk!

Adele Milk? Oh yes, I'll get it.

Rose What's the matter with the pair of you? It's on the tray. So you were saying . . .

Adele You see, I really admired what you both did in the war that –

Grace Would you please just pour the tea?

Adele does so.

Rose How do you know what I did in the war? Are you writing a book or something?

Grace That's exactly it. She wants to do some interviews with us for her book, isn't that right, Adele?

Adele Yes.

Grace And she's more than happy to help out until you feel up to answering her questions, unless of course you have any objections to that?

Rose If I find you're lying to me, I'll wrench your arm off and beat you to death with the soggy end.

Grace You'd be better off saving those sentiments for the low life who reduced you to needing us to stay in the first place.

She switches on the television. Hymn: 'Glorious Things of Thee are Spoken'.

Now, if you don't mind, I'd like to watch this free of interruption or interrogation.

Rose Are you both staying?

Grace Yes, indeed.

Rose For how long?

Grace As long as it takes.

Rose I think I'll just go and have little lie down.

Adele and Grace go to help her.

Rose Thanks, I can manage. (*She wheels herself off.*)

Adele I thought you said –

Grace I thought better of it. It all seemed to be a bit too much at once.

Adele Yes, I suppose so.

Grace I trust you have no objections?

Adele No, of course not. (*She tentatively sits down.*)

Grace The washing up?

Adele (*standing up*) Yes, of course. (*She takes the tray and goes.*)

SCENE FIVE

The beep, beep of the machine can be heard. Adele leaves the tray and puts her coat on and goes over to the bed.

Adele It took some getting used to. Honestly, God, I was so homesick. Not that I disliked Watford. In fact I rather took to it. I was expecting to see the same awful shops you seem to get everywhere but I got pulled up short when I saw that Laura Ashley was still alive and kicking. I started to feel quite at home.

I still secretly pined for my own house and fretted about the state of my flowerbeds, but when Grace did allow me to go home for a day or so, I found I couldn't settle. I didn't even want to go into the garden in case I missed Grace's call to summon me back. In that respect it was like having an affair. I could think of nothing else. It consumed my self whole. I so needed Rose and Grace's approval but most of all I still wanted more than anything to be one of them.

SCENE SIX

*Brett's living room. Brett, Luke and Melissa stare at the
old, battered cash box. They are surrounded by empty
cans of lager. They are playing strip-Happy Families.
Brett has his socks, pants and trousers on. Luke has only
his socks and boxer shorts on.*

Melissa (*puts her card down*) Mrs Bun, the baker's wife –
Go on get your boxers off –

Luke (*takes one of his socks off*) I'll stand here bollock-
naked if I have to before I touch that tin.

Brett (*pushing Melissa*) Go on yourself, Miss Mouthy –

Melissa I'm not touching it. Might be a dead baby's
skeleton.

Brett Come here and keep me warm then. (*He tries to
grab her.*)

Melissa Get off. Okay, I'll do it. (*Grabs the rusty screw
driver used to puncture the cans and tries to open the
box with it.*) Stand back – get back. In case –

Luke What?

*Melissa prises the box open but hesitates before
touching any of the contents, which are wrapped in
tissue paper.*

Brett What is it?

Melissa I'm not touching anything inside. Probably
crawling with germs.

Brett (*American accent*) Like you know dick. She don't
know dick, does she Luke?

His phone rings. It's a text message.

Luke (*American accent*) Na, na she wouldn't know dick if her goddam washing was hanging off it.

Melissa Here we go.

Brett Soon will though, eh?

Melissa You can shut up about that.

Brett You know the rule, you want to hang out with us you either fight us or you play nicely with me in the bedroom. (*He grabs her.*)

Melissa Luke, tell him –

Brett You want to really, don't you? Really?

Melissa Only in my nightmares.

Luke (*tentatively unwraps one of the packages and finds the broken glass*) One broken glass.

Brett (*letting Melissa go*) Yeah, yeah like that's worth shit.

Melissa Not now it's broken.

Brett Remember Paige. (*He grabs her hand and a piece of the broken glass as if he's about to cut her hand with it.*) You got that coming, if you don't deliver the goods. That's right Luke, isn't it?

Melissa (*wanting to distract Brett. To Luke*) What's that?

Luke (*unwrapping the next package*) It's some sort of medal.

Brett Told you.

Melissa Might be worth something.

Brett Every old gerry's probably got one of them.

Luke (*unwraps an SS dagger*) Look at this.

Brett What is it?

Luke Thought you weren't interested.

Brett (*picking up the dagger*) That'll do nicely.

Luke Excuse me?

Brett You can have that medal thing.

Luke I don't want the medal.

Melissa Aren't we going to try and sell them?

Brett Na, I'm keeping it.

Melissa Why don't we try and find out if they're worth anything first?

Brett (*about the knife*) It's only worth something to me. That's why I'm keeping it.

Melissa You don't know that for sure.

Brett You want to know how much it's worth. I'll show you how much it's worth. (*He starts to go.*)

Melissa Where you going?

Brett You want to ask those sort of questions you better act more like my girlfriend.

Melissa If you had a girlfriend she'd run a mile from you. You want me to do that?

Brett Like you've got anywhere to go. It's my place. I pay for it. Look what you're wearing, those shoes. Like you're going to get far in those – but like I saw you pay for them? No. You take what you want from me except the one thing I really want to give you. So you better think carefully before mouthing off about how you won't take me.

Rose's flat. Grace and Rose.

Grace *Ça va bien aujourd'hui, cherie?*

Rose You what?

Grace *Est-ce que –*

Rose My poor old mum died in fifty-eight. I haven't had any need to speak French since then.

Grace *Tu sais très bien c'est comme remonter une bicyclette.*

Rose So what if it's like riding a bicycle. I haven't ridden one of them since the war. And I don't intend to start again now.

Grace *Mais –*

Rose Aren't you missing your own home?

Grace It'll still be there when this is over.

Rose It is over. Grace, look at me. I'm better. I was able to tick every box on the district nurse's form about being ambulant in every room and now I've got the bath-rail I'm laughing.

Grace I wouldn't exactly say that.

Rose I'm sure you wouldn't –

Grace We thought everything would be the same after the war didn't we?

Rose The war? God, Grace – get out of the Tardis! For Christ's sake. The bloody war!

Grace But it wasn't. It was irrevocably changed.

Rose Good job and all.

Grace Just the same.

Rose You've just said it was changed. Irrevocably.

Grace I meant you. You always seemed to make a point of holding opposing views to me on practically everything in life.

Rose I didn't make a point of anything. What are you on about?

Grace And then flaring up at the least little thing –

Rose Your trouble is you can never acknowledge that there is another point of view.

Grace Always getting annoyed with me.

Rose I'm not annoyed with you. Now pass the paper and let's see what's on the box.

Grace Not that you were ever as cross with me as I was with you that day on the train to Lyon.

Rose Now what are you on about?

Grace That German guard. Don't you remember? The one who was very suspicious of my accent?

Rose Yes. Yes. It was so stupid our papers saying we were sisters when I sounded like an onion-growing peasant and you sounded like a direct descendant of Marie-Antoinette.

Grace She was Austrian.

Rose So?

Grace So how could my accent compare with hers?

Rose She must have learnt French to tell them all to eat cake. I bet it wasn't so much her saying, 'Let them eat cake', but the way she said it. I for one would be more than happy to live off cakes.

Grace Much good has it done you.

Rose It has actually. My GP reckoned I'd just have been an oozing blot on the carpet when you found me if I'd been thin. Lying in one place, you see, causes the equivalent of bedsores which eat at the flesh and cause it to leak away into a pond of septic pus.

Grace You came out with an equally gruesome story to that guard.

Rose What? I'd never heard of bedsores then. I'd probably have imagined it was another name for love-bites.

Grace You told him that my cut-glass accent was because I was suffering delusions – *folie de grandeur*, I think were your exact words – due to a terminal case of tertiary syphilis.

Rose Oh that, you're not still up in the air about that? Don't you see I was trying to save you from being raped?

Grace You probably saved me from being shot. No, I'm very grateful.

Rose You weren't at the time. In fact I think you'd have rather been shot than have anyone think you were a frowsy tart from Hertfordshire with VD.

Grace I have never minded in the least what people thought of me.

Rose No? What about what's-his-name? That poor boy in the Resistance when we were in that village – what was it called – just outside Lyon.

Grace Parc. What boy?

Rose Well – young man. Must have been twenty-five. Baby face, floppy reddish hair, big brown eyes, about five foot eight. You remember – who showed us every short cut in the traboules.

Grace Vaguely.

Rose Vaguely? He used to stand outside your bedroom door every night trying to build up the courage to knock. (*remembering*) Jean-Claude.

Grace Oh him. But when he heard you telling the others about what you'd said on the train to get us out of a spot, he never came near my room again. Just in case it was true.

Rose If you'd laughed about it he would have known it was a joke, but because you took offence he thought it might be true. You could have had such fun –

Grace Fun? We weren't there to have fun.

Rose laughs.

We weren't.

Rose You, you always were so . . . I don't know . . . starchy.

Grace One of us had to be alert and organised. And just as well, because do you remember what you were doing when –

Rose Don't –

Grace You don't know what I was going to say.

Rose I can guess. When I was outside the safe house washing my smalls which in my case never were –

Grace What?

Rose Small.

Grace It wasn't what you were washing, it was the fact that you were loudly humming 'Land of Hope and Glory'. Rose –

Adele comes in from outside carrying a weekend bag and a large cake box tied with ribbon.

Adele It's just me.

Grace So it is.

Adele I've brought us all a nice little something. (*She puts the box in Rose's lap.*)

Rose (*undoing the ribbon*) Adele, you must be a mind reader!

Grace (*to Adele*) Rose's key.

Holds out her hand. Adele gives her the key.

Rose Where did you –?

Adele I made a little detour via that scrummy patisserie in St Albans.

Grace Some detour.

Adele I'm sorry, I'm a bit –

Rose (*opens the box*) Grace, would you look at these? Look there's a *millefeuille caramelise* and a *tartelette bourdaloue* and – oh look at them . . . What's this one called?

Grace I've no idea.

Rose Cheer up, you po-faced old sod. *Barquette aux marrons*! Go on, have one. Look, a *religiesue aux fruits exotiques* – that's got your name on. Oh, and a *forêt noire*. My favourite. I haven't seen one of those for years, half a century probably.

Adele I'm surprised they were available in the war.

Rose You'd be amazed at what you could get your hands on in Lyon's traboules, eh Grace?

Grace I wouldn't know, I'm sure.

Adele Entertaining here was an absolute nightmare. Queuing at the butchers hoping that a bit of make up and a trembly lipped smile would get you an extra bit of sausage. That and a pig's heart and, phew, you knew you were home and dry.

Stops. The other two are staring at her.

Faggots. You see. That's what we called them then – meatballs. (*Attempts a joke.*) Queer name I know.

No response.

I'll put the kettle on then, shall I?

Rose No, no just sit down for a minute. Have you brought a pad?

Adele Pardon?

Rose Grace, bless her, has got me in the mood this afternoon, so why don't we crack on?

Adele On what?

Rose I do hope your dictation isn't as slow. Do you want to interview me for your book or have you changed your mind?

Adele Er . . . yes, okay. (*Rummages in her handbag and gets out a biro and a scrappy piece of paper.*)

Rose My mother was French and very proud of it. So I grew up speaking both French and English. Please feel free to interrupt with any questions.

Adele Thank you, but please carry on –

Rose But I wasn't able to read and write in the language. I left school at fourteen, unlike Grace and most of the rest who –

Grace Rose –

Rose I'm not ashamed of it. The only time I felt humiliated was when your lot used to pass round notes in Latin.

Grace She's not writing a book.

Rose She's not? Then what the Hell is she . . . ? (*to Adele*) What are you doing here then?

Adele As I sort of tried to say before, I admired you –

Grace She admired us so much she toured the country as an honoured guest speaker after the war. Would probably still be doing it now had I not happened to have been invited to one of the same events – a rather grand and very well attended Rotary Club dinner where I witnessed first-hand the frighteningly inaccurate talk about her so-called work in the French section of the Special Operations Executive.

Rose (*to Adele*) What was your code name?

Grace Cowardy Custard.

Rose (*to Adele*) I'm sorry, I don't remember you.

Grace Of course you don't! It was all poppycock. I doubt if she so much as knitted a pair of socks towards the war effort. She didn't even do her research properly. She maintained she was parachuted into France out of a Spitfire which everyone knows is impossible parachute from. It's a wonder she didn't claim she'd baled out of Thunderbird Four.

Rose laughs.

Adele (*gets up*) I'm sorry. If you'd rather I go –

Grace (*to Adele*) You stay here. (*to Rose*) I don't know how you can laugh in the face of such treachery – not only of us, but of those of us who didn't make it back. Those who were starved and tortured and who died in agony at the hands of the Gestapo rather than betray their friends. Freddie and Lance in Buchenwald and Michele and Marie who didn't even make it to Ravensbruck and –

Rose Fair do's. And I didn't mean to laugh at you, Adele. Were you mentally ill at the time?

Adele No, no, I don't think so.

Grace She did it because she wanted to be the centre of attention.

Rose (*to Adele*) But what has it got to do with you being here now?

Adele The guilt never left me. For years I wanted to find Grace again and ask her if there was some way I could make amends. When I read that there was going to be a memorial service in Southwark Cathedral for Lord Bartholomew, I guessed she'd be there.

Rose Barty's do, oh yes. Mind, wasn't Barty a pain in the proverbial?

Grace Rose.

Rose He was. Patronising little creep. He went to one of those boys' schools where they got their kicks by trying to hang themselves in the toilets on Saturday mornings.

Adele That erotic strangling thingy syndrome?

Grace That's quite enough.

Rose Didn't you ever wonder why the others were laughing so much at the Christmas get-togethers when the lucky dip was rigged so that he always got a soap on a rope?

Grace Barty was a brave man.

Rose It's easy to be brave when you risk your neck on a weekly basis giving yourself your best shot.

Rose laughs. Grace gives her a stern look.

Rose Even so, yes, he did a lot of good in occupied France and if you remember I was about to go to the memorial. I had my coat on and everything, then they came bursting – anyway, what has this got to do with Adele and why she's here?

Grace She came to Barty's memorial and reintroduced herself to me.

Rose Now, that is brave.

Adele I offered to give her a lift here. And I did what I could to help because I've always felt very badly for being so shallow and stupid as to pretend that I was one of you. And I wanted to make up for it before it was too late.

They both look at her.

Well, we're none of us getting younger.

Rose No. I see, and thank you. You've looked after me very well but I'm better now. And you've just spent two days in your own home. So why have you bothered to come back?

Grace Well, because –

Rose Excuse me. I'm talking to Adele.

Adele Grace asked me to.

Grace The fact of the matter is –

Rose (*ignoring Grace*) Adele?

Adele Helping you was just the first part of my penance.

Rose Really? So what was the second?

Adele Grace is going to teach me the skills I would have gained.

Rose What? What on earth for?

Adele For the third and final part.

Rose Which is?

Grace That we track down and put the fear of God Almighty into the scum who did this to you.

Rose (*laughs and laughs and laughs*) How can I ever stay annoyed with you? You are such a tonic.

Adele and Grace look at her in stony silence.

Rose I've rumbled you, haven't I? This is a game, isn't it? My G.P. or the district nurse or someone told you to test my long-term memory or something.

Grace No. I'm serious.

Rose You always are. But you can't mean it. You can't. Grace? Have you gone – ?

Grace What?

Rose Barking mad.

Grace Of course I haven't. What's barking about it? There was a time if someone had pissed on you, you'd have slit their throat.

Rose What would you know? One way or another people have pissed on me all my life. I've worked all my life since I left school and what have a got to show for it? Various boring bank jobs. One husband who died in the war. Another one who worked hard all his life and tried to rally after every lay-off and redundancy against the backdrop of your lot saying the unions have got too powerful. In the end it was a mixture of physical hard work and depression that made his heart give up. I'm only surprised that mine continues to keep beating.

Grace Are you sure it's your injuries that are preventing you from standing up straight or that chip on your shoulder?

Rose Excuse me. The only reason I got to work with you in the first place was that the French commies were fed up to the back teeth with the stuck up, toffee-nosed, public school, jolly-good-show arrogant English snobs in the Resistance.

Grace At least we got things done.

Rose You are so smug you still don't even bother to listen. You're simply content to sit there –

Grace I am not content to sit anywhere. All I want is justice. And in that respect I was never ever afraid to get my hands dirty. (*to Adele*) Are you still up for this?

Adele Oh, rather.

Grace (*to Rose*) How can you be so defeatist in front of this worthless woman who pretended to be you?

Rose I wonder how. Maybe the fact that I already own an NHS plastic hip, and have just returned from hospital after being beaten unconscious in my own home by three vicious, dead-eyed kids has something to do with it. Oh no, of course that is just a lily-livered, cowardly hypochondriac fantasy. It must just be that chip on my shoulder.

Grace I'm not suggesting we crawl and chop our way through the undergrowth with machetes. I mean finding out where they are and getting them to come to us.

Rose opens her mouth but words fail her. She shakes her head.

Just think about it, just for a moment. We tracked down people in an area much bigger than this and in a foreign country.

Rose You don't think the fact that they wore distinctive uniforms and spoke a different language gave us a bit of an advantage?

Grace But you told the police that you got a good look at your assailants and that you'd recognise them again.

Rose Yes, and why do you think I did that? Because it's their job to catch them.

Grace But what have they come up with – nothing. Meanwhile those dirty little brutes are out there somewhere, laughing, laughing their heads off. How dare they. How dare they think they've got away with it. And how can you just sit there and let them?

Rose Watch me.

Grace No, I don't want to. (*She gets up.*)

Rose Where are you going?

Grace Out. To find them.

Rose And how do you think you're going to do that?

Grace By asking people.

Rose You can't just go out on this estate running off at the mouth about criminals.

Grace Watch me.

Rose Don't be silly.

Grace I thought we'd already established that I'm never silly.

Rose Sit down. All right, I'll listen to what you have to say but I'm making no promises.

Grace (*to Adele*) Perhaps you'd be kind enough to take notes?

Adele Of course. Of course. Now we're cooking.

Grace (*ignores her. To Rose*) Just think about it, we do have certain skills and advantages.

Rose Where have you been? Who needs morse code with mobile phones? And we're too decrepit between us to switch one on.

Grace Our decrepitude is our most powerful weapon. No, let me finish. We are three wrinkled-up old dears. No one will ever suspect us of anything more sinister than being smelly or ga-ga or cheating at bingo.

Rose The next time you play bingo will be the first.

Adele I wouldn't mind trying it.

Grace (*ignoring her*) Whether it's bingo or whist, you know it's true. *Si nous unisons nos efforts nous pouvons le faire, juste comme autrefois.*

Adele Excuse me?

Grace Yes?

Adele I've lost you. What did you just say?

Grace *Si nous unisons –*

Adele What's that in English? I can't speak French.

Grace Let me get this straight. You pretended to have been parachuted behind enemy lines and to work with the French Resistance and you can't even speak the language?

Rose Grace, you've established she's a liar – now please leave her alone.

Grace She's got a French name!

Adele Actually it's German.

They look at her.

Adela – it means noble.

Grace snorts with derision.

Not that I am.

Grace You can say that again!

Adele I mean German. My parents just liked the name.

Rose Grace, calm down. She can hardly be expected to help or join in if she doesn't understand what you're saying. And you know what I feel about it. So I think you'd better pack the French in.

Grace (*to Rose*) As you wish.

Rose So?

Grace I know we have little to go on, but please, please, let's just try. Is there anything, anything you can think of which might give us a lead? Don't look at me like that. I didn't claim to have any miracles up my sleeve.

Rose There was.

Grace What?

Rose Something I didn't tell the police.

Grace Which was?

Rose The two SS officers who caught me humming 'Land of Hope and Glory'.

Grace Yes.

Rose It was their stuff. I kept it in an old tin box in the bottom of the wardrobe. They took that.

Adele Why didn't you tell the police?

Rose I didn't want to own up to it – having Nazi memorabilia.

Adele Why not? Surely you won it fair and square in the war, as it were.

Rose I just didn't really want to go into it all.

Adele How did you get it from the SS officers?

Grace She disposed of them.

Adele How do you mean?

Rose I shot one and slit the other's throat.

Adele You –?

Grace (*to Adele*) When you've watched the light go out of someone's eyes because of your own hand you don't start queuing up to talk about it at dinner parties. (*to Rose*) Can you remember exactly what was in it?

Rose Oh yes.

Grace (*to Adele*) You write this down.

Rose A small brandy glass with a swastika on it, a Knight's Cross, and an SS dagger.

Adele starts to shake as she writes. The bleep, bleep, bleep of the life support machine can be heard.

SCENE EIGHT

Brett's living room. Melissa and Luke run in. Melissa is carrying a copy of 'Medal News'. Sound of the shower. Brett's mobile phone is in the room and ringing.

Melissa (*to the phone*) Shut up. (*to Luke*) Where is he?

Luke Brett? (*Listens.*) He's in the shower.

The phone stops ringing.

Melissa Good. Let's hope he's ages.

Luke He's alright.

Melissa He's a psycho.

Luke I wouldn't have got out of Feltham alive if it weren't for him.

Melissa (*about the magazine*) Now you'll be able to pay him off.

Luke I don't want to pay him off. He's my best mate.

Melissa Yeah, yeah, yeah. So?

Luke What?

Melissa You want to – you know – while he's not here.

Luke Suppose he comes in?

Melissa Make it more exciting.

Luke You sure?

Melissa I'm up for it if you are.

Luke Shotgun first?

Melissa I don't need to but you go ahead if it makes you feel better.

Luke (*picks up a can of lager*) Sure?

Melissa Yeah. (*Waves it away.*) Did you bring something with you?

Luke In my pocket.

Melissa (*about the can*) Put that down then and put it on.

Luke Do you want to watch a video first?

Melissa No, we don't need that. We know how to do it, don't we?

Luke If Brett comes in we'll act like we've been running. (*Takes a CD out of his pocket and puts it in the player.*)

Melissa Hurry up.

Luke I'm putting it on. I'm putting it on.

*Diana Ross singing 'Chain Reaction'. They start
to dance to the movements they've obviously
choreographed together, à la Pan's People. Brett's
mobile phone starts ringing. Melissa picks up the
phone.*

Luke Don't.

Melissa (*looks at the phone*) It's someone called Dave.

Luke Is it a message?

Melissa No. Shall I answer it?

Brett comes in, wrapped in a towel.

Brett Get that crap music off. (*Switches music off, goes
to his phone.*) What are you doing with that?

Melissa Nothing. Who's Dave?

Brett This guy, this mate of mine –

Melissa Yeah? What's he do?

Brett Works over the parks –

Melissa How come I've never met him?

Brett 'Cos you ain't my mother. You aren't even part of
this gang, you've not been blooded. Keep your nose out.
In fact get out. Just get out.

Melissa Yeah? Right then, and I'm taking this with me.

Brett Have it. Have it.

Luke Brett, don't let her go. It's worth something.

Brett She won't get far. Her mum don't want her back.
Social Services will slap her straight into secure care.
Where's she going to go?

Luke Brett.

Brett (*to Melissa*) What's it worth, then?

Melissa (*showing him the magazine*) It's called a Knight's Cross. It says in good condition one can fetch eight hundred pounds.

Brett Yeah?

Luke (*takes the magazine from her*) She's telling the truth. Look, look, it's German.

Brett That old smelly gerry was a Nazi.

Luke (*looking through the magazine*) There's addresses and stuff at the back where you can send them or – look, get it auctioned.

Melissa Like we should turn up with stolen stuff and then tell them to send the money to our address?

Brett She's right. We've got to flog it to a dildo who don't ask goddam questions.

Melissa There's no shortage of them round here.

Brett But you know what this means?

Luke What?

Brett That lots of old scroungers must have shit loads of this type of stuff just sitting in the bottom of their wardrobes.

Melissa You reckon?

Brett Selling this is not the end. This is just the beginning. We will rob them on the estates, We will mug them in their sheltered housing, in their nursing homes, at the bus stops, on the streets, and in the parks. Until we emerge rich and victorious!

End of Part One.

Part Two

SCENE NINE.

Rose's flat. An enlarged copy of the Watford street plan mounted on cardboard is hanging on the wall. Next to it are pencil drawings of Brett, Luke and Melissa. Grace stands next to it. Rose and Adele, note pad in hand, sit facing her.

Grace Our objective is to find these three thugs who attacked Rose. We think –

Adele Am I required to write that down?

Rose Of course not.

Grace Was your claim to be able to do shorthand a lie also?

Adele No, no.

Grace Then you've no excuse not to write down every word that's been said.

Rose Grace – really! As if we don't know what our objective is.

Grace Very well. (*With a ruler, points to the pictures of the gang.*) Of course, for all we know they may live on the Isle of Wight or have fled the country, but the probability is that they live within a three-mile radius. And –

Rose We've already agreed all this and done the surveillance.

Grace It doesn't do any harm to re-cap.

Rose Come on now Grace, it's not as if we've got Alzheimer's. Touch wood. (*She knocks on the table or something wooden twice. Beat.*) Come in.

Rose and Adele laugh.

Adele Should I write that down?

Grace No.

Rose I was just having a bit of a giggle. Go on.

Grace The one thing we know for sure is that they took some objects which could be sold for quite a considerable amount of money, but I have traipsed around every antique shop, second-hand shop and junk shop in the whole of Watford. I sweet-talked them, offered them bribes, the lot, but I'm fairly certain that none of the items were offered in any of the shops round here.

Rose How many more times, they were just ignorant kids. They wouldn't have had any idea what the stuff was worth. They thought they'd got a cash box. When they found out there was no cash in it they probably chucked the whole lot in the canal.

Adele Or over a hedge.

Rose Left it outside the Oxfam shop, even.

Grace For all we know, one might have fallen on the knife and bled to death. Another might have swallowed the medal and choked on it and the third ground up the glass and sprinkled it on each of the other two's cornflakes.

Adele Oh, I think if something like that had happened, we'd have seen it on the news.

Rose Probably been the main item. (*then*) Sorry, Grace, what were you saying?

Grace How did you get on, Rose?

Rose Between us Adele and I watched every kid go in to every secondary school on the list but our friends didn't show.

Grace What about the Labour Exchange?

Rose For goodness sake.

Grace I mean the DHSS or whatever its name is now.

Adele No joy there either, I'm afraid.

Rose But we did find out that they don't play music in there so that sort of took the dairy off that film *The Full Monty*.

Adele We also found out that youths between the ages of sixteen and eighteen can't claim benefits anyway.

Grace So, what sort of other things would they be likely to do?

Rose shrugs.

What about discos?

Adele What about them?

Grace Young people seem to frequent them.

Adele Oh, I thought you meant the crisps for a moment. You mean clubs. There's that big one.

Rose Pringles?

Grace Where's that?

Rose They sell them in tubes in the supermarket.

Grace looks at her.

They're big crisps. (*then*) Forget it.

Grace Rose, please.

Rose (*to Adele*) Do you mean The Area?

Adele I think so.

Grace Is it or isn't it?

Rose What?

Grace In the operations area?

Rose That's what it's called. The name of the club – The Area. They all queue up outside to get in on Saturday nights.

Adele I know. Outside it says, 'A bit of Ibiza in Watford'.

Grace Right, you can go there.

Rose They'd never let her in.

Grace She could get a job there.

Rose They won't employ an OAP behind the bar.

Grace Who said anything about working behind the bar? She could do bottle-washing, clean the toilets –

Rose Be realistic.

Grace All right. She could wait outside and look at who goes in.

Rose It doesn't get going until midnight.

Grace So? Doing your ironing was not the main reason you came here, was it, Adele?

Adele Absolutely not, no.

Rose Even so. Grace, I'm sorry, and I really don't want to rain on your parade, but this is all hopeless.

There is a noise off at the front door. Rose stiffens and looks frightened. Adele gets up.

Rose Who's that?

Adele (*calls off*) Anyone there?

Rose (*to Grace, about her nervousness*) Sorry.

Adele (*bouncing back in, brandishing the 'Watford Observer'*) It's only the paper. Great thick thing.

Grace If I had to write a reference for her, those are just the adjectives I'd use.

Rose Grace.

Grace Yes?

Rose Please. (*then*) Why don't we divide it up? (*She gives a section to Adele.*)

Grace We haven't got time to sit and read –

Rose It's not beyond the realm of possibility that we might see my stuff for sale in the small ads.

Grace Give me a bit of it then. (*She takes a section and starts to read.*) Just listen to this. (*Reads.*) 'Mother you always showed us love and kindness, you was always fair. And we was taught to care with love few families can say they share.'

Adele (*looking at an article in her section*) Oh my word.

Grace Quite.

Rose What?

Adele There's a photo of some poor chap who's recovering in hospital after being robbed and attacked in his own home.

Grace I'm surprised it's considered news.

Rose Does it say how many of them there were?

Adele Three.

Grace That sounds familiar.

Adele It also says that when he protested they threatened him with a knife.

Rose Ah, but you see that didn't happen to me.

Adele He claims it was a dagger used by the SS in the Second World War.

Grace Where?

Adele It doesn't say but I would think it was somewhere in Germany.

Rose Can I see that?

Grace (*taking the paper*) Hollywell. At least we know they still have the knife. Although they'd be really stupid I suppose to hold on to it now.

Rose (*looking at the article*) This is dreadful. This is too terrible.

Grace At last you've come round to my way of thinking.

Rose How dare they?

Grace Do you think it would be worth talking to the old people in those flats?

Rose Definitely.

Adele If that's what you'd like me to do then –

Rose But you'll need a cover story – another persona. Someone they'd let in without question.

Adele Such as?

Grace You have twelve hours to think of something. We'll test you in the morning.

Brett's living room. Brett is cleaning a pair of shoes over the local paper. Melissa is carefully packing a collection of 1940s junk (a couple of medals, old ashtrays, broken radio, rations books, etc.) into a large holdall.

Brett How much d'you reckon?

Melissa Don't know.

Brett We got six hundred for that medal so . . .

Melissa But these others might be more common –

Brett Yeah, but even if they was only worth a hundred each. Them and all that other stuff – I reckon we're looking at, what, a couple of K minimum.

Melissa (*lifting the bag*) I don't think he'll be able to carry it all.

Brett We better go with him anyway in case he gets mugged on the way.

Melissa We can't all keep waltzing down there. People will get to know us, recognise us.

Brett We'll let Luke do the talking.

Melissa Set him up? So he's the one they'll remember?

Brett No. That's what the tash is for.

Melissa (*half-laugh*) Tash.

Brett Then after, right, you and me'll go out for a meal, yeah? No, I'm not talking burgers. I know places where they show you to the table.

Melissa Don't think –

Brett It won't mean nothing. It's just a meal.

Brett's phone rings. Luke, now sporting a moustache, comes in from the bedroom, dressed in a black suit, à la the gang in 'Reservoir Dogs' trying to do up a tie.

Luke Can someone help me with this?

Melissa goes to help Luke with the tie while Brett answers his phone.

Brett (*to phone, American accent*) Nah, that's not me. Na, I just bought this goddam phone from a dude down the High Street. Na, never heard of him. Don't call this number no more. (*Ends call. To Luke*) Let's have a look. There, you look like a real gent.

Luke Where's the shoes then? (*He goes over to them and starts to put them on.*)

Brett (*his phone rings again. Answers it*) Piss off. (*Ends call.*)

Melissa What are you talking about, that is your phone.

Brett I know that you know that but he don't know that. (*then*) Ready?

Luke I could still be identified.

Brett Not if you shave off the moustache straight after. If the bloke wants to shop you – which he won't 'cos he's making so much out of us – but if he did he'd describe you as a guy with a tash and by then you won't have one. Laughing.

Luke has finished putting his shoes on. He picks the newspaper up from the floor and stands up.

Melissa (*going up to Luke*) Don't take this the wrong way. I don't want to pull your manhood's from underneath you or nothing but even this close up the tash isn't noticeable.

Luke She's right.

Melissa (*takes out her mascara brush and starts to put mascara on the hair above Luke's lip*) Hold still.

Luke What you doing?

Brett She's just colouring it in a bit.

Melissa Yeah, trust me.

While she continues to colour in Luke's moustache, he idly looks at the paper in his hand and then sees the article.

Luke How come you never said anything about this?

Brett What?

Luke This – in the paper.

Melissa It's a photo of that skaggy old crumbly down the Hollywell flats.

Brett (*looks*) What's it say?

Luke Vicious gang of three.

Brett Hey, see that. We're famous.

Melissa (*reading over his shoulder and reading it*) It mentions the knife. The German knife. That's it, you have to get rid of it.

Brett No way.

Melissa Just let Luke show it to the bloke with this other stuff and ask how much it's worth.

Brett But now it's been in the paper he'll know for sure it's stolen.

Melissa He won't have seen this. He's from out of town.

Luke And he knew the Nazi medal was dodgy but he still took it.

Brett Whose side are you on?

Luke Yours. If you hang on to it, you'll get caught.

Melissa He's right.

Brett Can't you see it's lucky? It's already made us famous and we're about to become very rich.

Luke Yeah but –

Brett 'What's done is done, I need you cool. Are you cool?' Mr Pink?

Luke 'I'm cool, Mr Orange.'

Brett I ain't Mr Orange. I'm Joe Cabot.

Luke Sorry boss.

Brett That's better. 'Let's go to work.'

SCENE ELEVEN

Rose's living room. Grace sits at the table. Rose comes in with a tray of tea things and half a bottle of vodka.

Grace Are you sure you can manage all that?

Rose Just about. I'm beginning to think we should have taken her to a real café for her test.

Grace We have no idea how she'll behave. She might give the game away entirely. (*She pours the vodka into the teapot.*)

Rose Shouldn't we make it look a bit more convincing and boil the vodka in the kettle first?

Grace And let the alcohol evaporate? I should jolly well think not. This is seventy per cent proof.

Rose Now you're not going to make it completely impossible for her, are you?

Grace All she has to do is keep drinking the tea. And not call us by our real names.

Knock at the door.

Rose Just don't give her too hard a time. Come in.

Adele comes in dressed as a nun. They are both impressed.

Grace Good God –

Adele (*terrible Irish accent*) Well, top o' the morning to yous both. And how are we faring this fantastically fine morning? I'm Sister Maria, don't you know.

Grace How do you do, Sister Maria. I'm Matilda and this is my grand-niece, Tracy, who works as a waitress here.

Rose Hello, Sister. Sit down and have some tea.

Adele Now I don't mind if I do, so I don't. It's very kind of you to be sure, Matilda, Tracy. (*Sits down.*)

Grace The accent is inept. Drop it.

Adele Oh, do you think so? (*in response to a look from Grace*) Oaky-doky. (*Takes a mouthful of tea.*) What sort of tea is this?

Rose A tell-the-truth potion.

Adele It's cold.

Rose It works.

Grace looks at her.

Well, it is cold, innit? What d'you want?

Grace Rose?

Rose 'Scuse me. Name's Tracy, innit lady, and I'm supposed to be about sixteen and believe me that's their idea of being polite. (*to Adele*) So? What? You want something to eat or what?

Adele I wouldn't mind. What have you got?

Grace (*to Rose*) Let her have cake. Come on Sister Maria, drink up.

Rose goes to the kitchen to get the cake.

Adele (*drains the cup, which Grace then refills*) What is in it?

Grace Very exotic. Lapsang souchong or some such. I expect it's not what you're used to. Are you only allowed water in the convent?

Adele I don't live in a convent. That's all changed. Very few of us do any more. I live in the community.

Grace Really? What is your order?

Adele Well, I wouldn't have minded cheese on toast. Just joking. We're called The Little Sisters of Clemency.

Grace Drink up, Sister. And what exactly do you do?

Adele The spirit of the order is to befriend the lonely and aged. (*beginning to feel the effect of the alcohol*) To walk with them and talk with them along life's narrow way.

Grace Do you do anything specifically for them?

Rose comes back with a piece of cake.

Adele I try and help in what ever way I can. At the present time I'm trying to set up a reminiscence project. I'm collecting artefacts from the Second World War. So we can keep senility from the door with a bit of oral what do you call it, history. Do you know I nearly said sex.

Grace Did you indeed. (*She looks at Rose.*)

Adele But you wouldn't fail me on that, would you? I mean it might not be beyond the realm of possibility that it leapt from a nuns lips. It could be as much on a someone's mind who's never had it as for someone who had had a lot of it. (*She pours herself some more tea, takes several large sips.*)

Rose It's just that most people don't want it shoved down their throats. Cake?

Adele takes a cake.

Adele Thank you, my child.

Rose Pleasure, I'm sure. I went to a convent school, init.

Adele Did you, my child?

Rose And if you don't mind me saying I think you lot are all a load of bloody bitches.

Adele God be with you, my child.

Grace Tracy, perhaps you'd go out and make some coffee.

Adele Not for me. The tea's just dandy. I mean coffee would be an indulgence.

Rose Let me top you up. (*Does so.*)

Grace (*to Rose*) Steady on. (*to Adele*) Indeed? I expect obedience was the hardest vow for you to keep.

Adele Really, Matilda, you hardly know me. What makes you think that?

Grace I know it would be for me.

Adele Oh for you, yes, I can see that it would be for you but for me, no – the hardest one was chastity. (*Takes a large gulp of tea.*) Oh yes, for me, maintaining my

54

chastity has been a constant struggle with the devil which has left me wanting on many occasions. (*Swills down the rest of the tea.*)

Grace I'm wondering if perhaps this is too much information, Sister.

Rose Yeah, if you're such a randy fornicator how come you're still a religious sister?

Adele (*beat*) Because it was with a priest and they don't mind that so much. They call it 'keeping it in the family' and we weren't hurting anyone else. Although you could argue that I'd made a cuckold out of Jesus as technically I'm married to him.

Rose Seems to me that you and Jesus ain't no longer singing from the same hymn sheet.

Grace Yes, fascinating as this discourse might be, isn't it just a bit unlikely to be springing from the mouth of a nun?

Adele Maybe, but then I am a nun in a million. You see, along life's narrow way there are two big stumbling blocks if you don't include death. These are the dirty great boulders of money and sex. Too little of them can be ruinous and too much of them, too much of both of them can be, can be, can be – boring.

Grace It seems to me that we are now cavorting recklessly into the realms of inappropriateness.

Adele But that's just where you're incorrect. There is a part in every English woman's soul which longs for the convent life, no demands, no decisions about what to wear, no more silly naked performances with spouses to be got over before being able to finish the chapter of the book. In some women of course it is smaller than others but all of them will admire and revere my life-choice and open up to me. I will win their hearts and confidence with my modern, no nonsense, bold approach to life's big bollocks, bollards, err . . . rollocks, err, rocks.

Then, as Grace and Rose look as if they might interrupt her:

No, no, hear me out. I know what you're going to say, but I have answers for the younger generation as well. What they can't fathom is why there are so many gays. Of course we had them in our day – the gentlemen who could tell a pelmet from a helmet – but these days they're inundated with them. Young women are being shelved all over the place and they have no idea why. But the answer is staring them in the face, literally in the face. Purple and black lipstick is behind it. What man would want to kiss a mouth which looks like a vulva with hypothermia?

Grace Sister, Sister. The only thing we are now plumbing the depths of is vulgarity.

Adele I'm sorry. Tracilda and Macey. I mean Marilla and Pastry.

Grace Try as I might I cannot recall any advice on lipstick in any of the gospels.

Adele I'm sorry Hilda and Pacey. Sorry. I mean. I'm sorry, can we start again?

Grace Perhaps you'd like to wait in the bedroom, Sister, while I have a word with my colleague.

Adele Yes, of course, Marm. (*She staggers out.*)

Rose Don't start up about her, Grace.

Grace I was merely about to say that I think she'll do.

Rose You do?

Grace The woman's a natural-born liar. She's perfect.

Hospital.

Adele (*to God*) And, that is how, after I'd had a little lie
down in a darkened room with a couple of Anadin and
two gallons of water, I became a nun. I know, God, that
I wasn't called by you. I got the idea from a tourist leaflet
I'd picked up the day I bought the cakes. Apparently
St Alban had become a saint by exchanging clothes with
a fugitive priest and then been martyred in the priest's
place. And hey presto, there was my idea for a disguise.
I was so respected as a religious sister I let myself forget
that I hadn't earned it, and although I was still counting
magpies it was now one for other people's sorrow and
two for others' joy. There was no problem getting past
the front doors. People couldn't wait to get me into their
homes and to tell me their stories. A woman older than
myself whose husband had returned to her after being
released from a Japanese prisoner-of-war camp and then
proceeded to torture and abuse her for the rest of their
married life. I knelt with a woman who'd paid for her
daughter, her only child, to have a back-street abortion
in the 'sixties and her daughter had died days later of
septicaemia. Neither of them had told anyone in all
that time. Years of guilt and shame which had eaten
away at their spirit until, like me, when they reflected
on their lives they felt an empty nothingness.

(*to the bed*) I suppose that's what it's like for you now.
All this machinery. They can monitor and measure
everything except the soul. When I was a child I used to
think it was part of the body, shaped like a puffed-up
bird stuck behind the heart but that if it became stuffed
full of sins it would atrophy and then the Devil could
come and spear it with his pitchfork, whereupon it
would crumble apart like an empty wasps nest. Oh God,

now how I wish I'd never started it, or at least tried to stop it, or just that I'd run and run and got away from this hell I'd made.

SCENE THIRTEEN

Rose's living room. Graces fiddles with a radio cassette and appears to be taping a time check from the radio. Rose has a washing line and blindfold over her arm. She starts to undo the washing line. They both stop and stand still when they hear Adele opening the front door. Adele comes in laden down with shopping.

Adele Anyone for the cup that cheers?

As one Rose and Grace move forward and pin Adele to a chair.

Adele (*struggling*) What have I done? What have I done?

Grace Sit still and shut up.

Adele obeys and they blindfold her and tie her up.

Adele What, what are you doing? I've got some information for you.

Grace blindfolds Adele.

Rose This is no good.

Grace Looks fairly secure to me.

Rose But we hardly overpowered her, did we? And there are three of them, a quarter our age.

Adele Oh, I see. You were just practising on me. Jolly good.

Grace What have you got for us?

Adele Gave me a bit of a turn, I don't mind telling you.

Grace Perhaps you wouldn't mind telling us your information.

Rose takes Adele's blindfold off.

Adele I had quite a session today with one of the old boys who was burgled. Used to be the organist of his local church and take the choirboys camping.

Grace Spare us the details.

Adele Of course. I only wish I could have been spared them. Anyway he's housebound now, thank God. But his home-help told him that she thought she'd seen his stolen medals at one of those antique fair thingies in a church hall in Bushey. The old boy gave me some money and asked if I'd go and see if I could buy them back for him.

Grace So did you go?

Adele Yes.

Rose And?

Adele The stallholder gave me the medals back for a couple of quid and he readily admitted to having bought a Knight's Cross. Most importantly he's not as yet been offered the dagger but he knows they've got one because he heard them arguing about it and he thinks they might come back with it today.

Grace And you got all this out of him without arousing his suspicions?

Adele (*about the crucifix*) One of these swinging around your neck and everyone automatically believes that every word that comes out of your mouth is true. I told him I didn't want any fuss, that the kids involved were my sister's grandchildren but she would pay very well to get it back. I managed to get him to agree not to offer them anything for it today but tell them to come back on Sunday.

Rose Sunday?

Adele That's the last day of the fair.

Rose Doesn't give us much time.

Adele I can always go back –

Grace No, no. Sunday's fine.

Rose But Grace, even if we do manage to get them back here we still don't know how we'll overpower them.

Adele How about pepper? Flinging that in their faces.

Grace Too amateur –

Adele I know. Empty washing-up liquid bottles filled with lemon juice and aim at the eyes?

Grace No.

Rose But she's on the right track.

Adele What about a flare or something of that nature?

Rose A smoke bomb?

Grace C.S. gas maybe. But where to get –

Rose Mace spray.

Grace Yes.

Adele I don't think you can get that in Argos.

Rose No, but you can in France.

Grace Let's go.

Rose We can't just –

Grace To the travel agent. (*to Adele*) Come on, isn't this what you always wanted – to be on a secret mission in France?

Adele Yes, but I'm tied to the chair.

Rose (*starts to untie her*) So you are. You did very well today.

Adele Thank you.

Grace Eurostar.

Adele (*hearing this as 'you're a star'*) Do you really think so?

Grace Yes, Eurostar.

Adele (*beaming*) Thank you, Grace.

Rose I think she means the train that goes in the tunnel under the channel.

Grace Yes, let's ask them how much three OAP cheap day returns cost.

All three leave.

SCENE FOURTEEN

Brett's living room. Melissa, Brett and Luke. Luke has three cans of lager.

Brett We're not going round there tanked-up.

Melissa But we are going round there?

Luke I don't like it.

Brett Me neither.

Melissa A thousand quid, she said. What's there not to like?

Brett A nun tells the bloke that runs the stall that she knows someone who'll pay a thousand quid for the knife. So he gives us the address and it turns out to be the house we robbed it from in the first place.

Melissa So? If she wants it that bad we better get over there and collect the reward.

Luke (*pulling away*) It's too weird. You don't think that nun was working for the filth?

Melissa Like the police would have any truck with her. Get real.

Brett But why would she want to pay to get her own stuff back? Why not tell the cozzers?

Melissa It's like the bloke on the stall told you, it's illegal to own it. She'd be as much in the shit as we would, dick-brain.

Brett You'd do well to remember Paige.

Melissa What did happen to her?

Luke She got ripped. Like out of a book.

Melissa You already been on the piss?

Brett Rip as in R.I.P.

Melissa You're all talk, you are. All that stuff. All those smeggie, gerry flats we broke into and it was all for nothing. Make us rich? You was talking out of your arse as per usual.

Brett Right, right. You're happy enough to play shotgun with my lager, doss down here 'cos no one else can stand the sight of you. Whose money bought them shoes, that top? Come on, take them off. Let's have them back then.

He tries to grab her but she avoids him.

You don't want to give them back? So right, you listen to me, the next time you open your mouth is to give me head. Got it? I've got to get out of here.

He shoves her and then storms out.

Melissa Thanks for helping me out there. Not.

Luke (*offering her a lager*) He wasn't to know the other stuff was worthless.

Melissa Fine, but now we know we can get good money for the knife and he won't sell it.

Brett's phone rings. Melissa picks it up.

Luke Leave it.

Melissa (*to phone*) Hello. (*then*) Yes, he is. (*to Luke*) It's for you.

Luke Me? Is it Brett? (*Takes the phone.*)

Melissa Don't think so.

Luke Hello. Yeah. Yeah, I'm Luke, but I don't know you. No, I'm not pretending.

Melissa (*hisses*) Who is it?

Luke (*shrugs*) Dunno. (*to phone*) Who are you? What d'you want?

Melissa Drugs?

Luke So, okay just remind me. What is the usual? (*Pause.*) No. You got the wrong number, mate. (*Ends the call.*)

Melissa So was it drugs?

Luke shakes his head.

Thought not. Brett couldn't manage to get anyone sorted with anything harder than a Prittstick. How come they asked for you anyhow?

Luke Dunno.

Melissa I do. Whatever he's doing, he's doing it with your name.

Brett comes back in. They look at him.

Brett Forgot my phone. (*then*) What?

Melissa What you pretending to be him for?

Brett What you on about now?

Luke She answered the phone and someone asked for me so I spoke to them.

Brett What did they want?

Luke The usual.

Melissa The usual what?

Brett You told her?

Luke shakes his head.

Melissa Told me what?

Brett I've been thinking about what you were saying and okay, we'll go round there with the knife.

Luke But I thought you said you were never going to part with it.

Brett Who said anything about parting with it? And after, right, when we've got the money we'll go to The Area, right? (*to Melissa*) That's what you want isn't it? A proper date? (*Puts on 'I Gotcha'.*) You want to dance? (*Starts to dance.*)

Melissa What were you making out to be him for?

Brett Come on. I wasn't. Sometimes we just use each other's names don't we, Luke?

Luke That's right, Luke.

64

Brett See. (*to them both*) C'mon then. Let's have shotgun and a bit of a Pan's People show before we go, eh?

He gets them both to dance. Then:

Come on. Let's go to work.

SCENE FIFTEEN

Rose's living room. Sunday evening. Grace, who is wearing a Winston Churchill mask, is standing on a small stepladder, looking out of the window. She gives a signal to Adele, who is wearing a Madonna mask, and Rose, who is wearing an Elton John mask. They go through their choreographed routine. Adele goes to the kitchen and switches on the kettle. Rose opens the window and checks that the front door isn't locked and then stands behind it. Grace gets down from the ladder, switches off the light and hides somewhere else in the room so she's facing the widow or the door. The kettle boils. They all stand in unison and point their mace sprays at the kitchen door.

Grace Excellent. (*She goes back to her lookout point.*)

Rose Except they're leaving it a bit late. I thought you said they were really excited –

Adele They were –

Rose (*about the mask*) Mine's really itchy. Is yours?

Adele It's rather hot. It hasn't got as big nostrils as Churchill's.

Grace For the last time, do you want to swap?

Rose Not with bloody Churchill.

Adele I do like the look of this one but it doesn't immediately jump out at you as Marilyn Monroe.

Rose At least it makes you look glamorous.

Grace If they don't turn up this evening, I'll take you both to the shop tomorrow and you can choose what you like.

Rose I thought you said they didn't have much choice.

Grace They didn't.

Rose Not again. We'll all be worn out.

Grace This is real. They've just come around the corner.

They put on their masks and go though the routine again. Brett tries the front door. It opens.

Brett It was open.

Melissa No one leaves their front door open at night.

Brett lifts the window and goes in followed by Luke and Melissa.

Brett Go on, go in her bedroom.

Melissa Why me?

Brett We can't, we're blokes.

Melissa So? Ain't you been in a woman's bedroom before?

Brett Not one so disgusting and wrinkly her hair falls out on the pillow.

Luke Shush.

Melissa Huh, you haven't been in none, have you, young or old? That's it isn't it? You aren't a pusher. Why didn't I think of it before. You're a renter.

Brett You did tell her.

Luke No.

Melissa All that talk about having me. What a joke, you wouldn't know where to start.

The kettle starts to boil.

Luke Shush, listen.

Melissa What?

Luke The kettle.

Brett She's in the kitchen.

Brett, Melissa and Luke go into the kitchen. Rose flicks on the light in the living room. Grace and Adele stand up and all three point their sprays at the kitchen door as Brett Luke and Melissa come out again. All three of them use their sprays on the gang. However Adele's is facing the wrong way and she sprays herself. Rose turns to see what's happened. Grace sprays Melissa. As Rose turns back, Brett kicks the can from Rose's hand but in doing so he drops the knife. He and Luke manage to get back out of the window. Melissa is left screaming on the floor. The women take their masks off. Rose goes over to her.

Grace (*to Adele*) You idiot. Can't you do anything right?

Adele I'm sorry. I'm so sorry.

Melissa (*writhing on the floor as Rose tries to tie her up*) My eyes, my nose. I can't breathe! (*to Adele*) Help me Madonna, help me.

Rose (*spraying her again*) Hold still and shut up. I said shut up.

Grace This is so, so tiresome.

Adele I'm sorry – let me – is there anything I can do?

Melissa (*to Adele*) Save me, Madonna. Please stop them.

Grace (*to Adele*) Just get out of my sight.

Adele goes.

Grace This is a fine how-do-you-do.

Rose Stop whining and help me tie this one up.

Grace I'm not sure what you hope to achieve?

Rose Information. She wasn't the one who urinated on me. I want to know where to find the other two.

Melissa You won't find out from me.

Rose (*laughs*) Famous last words.

Grace By the time we've finished with you, you'll be pleading with us just to put you out of your misery.

Adele alone. Bleep, bleep, bleep noise.

Adele I had well and truly fallen from Grace. I was shaking, even more frightened than the day when Grace had asked me to take notes and Rose had told me what she'd done in the war. I had to do everything I could to get back into their good books. God, you see that, don't you? Between them they hatched a plan and decided that they needed something that looked like the male member – Well, just let's say that I was able to convince them that a chipolata wouldn't look realistic enough and what they really needed was a nice bit of turkey neck. I don't know if they thought my expertise came from my exploits with butchers during the war, or that it was more to do with my familiarity with the real thing. As it turned out you can no longer get turkey neck in the butchers, you have to go to a pet shop, so I was gone a while. I'm not sure what they did to the girl but I know they kept plunging her head in the sink until she begged them to stop believing that her lungs were bursting. Then with the recorded hourly time checks which they played every twenty minutes they managed to thoroughly confuse her about how long she'd been there and after a very short while the sound of a tap being turned on and off was enough to make her scream.

Grace, Rose and Melissa, who is still blindfolded and tied to a chair.

Grace (*putting a partly filled bucket of water down on the floor*) Well, it doesn't look like your friends are coming back for you?

Melissa People will know I'm missing. They'll find me.

Rose Really? How many people did you tell you were coming to rob an old woman? And even if you had, I don't suppose you have anyone who's bothered enough to come looking for you.

Grace No, because you're nothing.

Melissa Please, please just let me go.

Rose Let you go? After we've gone to all this trouble. I don't think so.

Melissa What are you going to do with me?

Rose We're going to do to you what you did to me.

Melissa It wasn't me.

Rose It would be better for you if you didn't lie, especially about what we already know.

Melissa It wasn't mainly me. It was Brett.

Rose But you were with him, weren't you? I didn't hear you trying to stop him.

Melissa Go on then, beat me up, piss on me, rob me. Please just get it over with.

Grace Only, you see, my friend nearly died.

Melissa But she didn't, did she?

Grace (*switches the tape recorder on. The sound of gas escaping*) No, because I found her in time. But none of your friends have come to save you. No one will find you.

Melissa What's that noise? What's that noise.

Grace (*to Rose*) I can't hear anything can you?

Rose Not a dickie bird. Pass the matches would you?

Melissa No. It's gas! It's gas!

Rose squirts some lighter fuel up Melissa's nose.

Melissa (*screams*) What's that? What's that?

Grace We thought you young people liked putting funny smelling stuff up your nose.

Melissa (*sniffing*) But it's petrol!

Grace No, this is petrol. (*She flings the water from the bucket over Melissa.*)

Melissa (*screams*) You can't . . . You'd never get away with it.

Grace (*going over to the door*) What do we care? We're old.

Rose (*follows Grace to the door*) It doesn't matter to us if we spend the rest of our lives in prison. In fact it's toe-rags like you who have made home prison for people like me.

Grace In fact I'm quite looking forward to it. We'll be safe and have all our meals cooked for us.

Rose (*shaking the matchbox*) Umm, shall I light the gas?

Melissa What is it you want to know? Just ask me and I'll tell you anything.

Rose and Grace go back over to Melissa.

Grace Now I do believe that we might be getting somewhere.

Rose We need you to tell us everything.

Melissa And then you'll let me go?

Rose Yes. But only if everything goes according to plan.

Melissa But –

Grace You have no choice at all. If you double-cross us we'll kill you.

SCENE SIXTEEN

Brett's living room. Brett and Luke stagger in, paralytic.

Brett You saw it, didn't you – right out of her hand and across the room.

Luke You're something else, you know that, Luke.

Brett Yeah. Get the light, Luke.

Luke (*flicks the switch, nothing happens*) Busted.

> *Goes to radio/CD player turns it on. It throws out some light and music.*

Brett Power cut. (*Tries to kick the light switch and slightly overbalances.*)

Luke (*holding him up*) Can't be. Sounds work. Brett?

Brett What?

Luke I mean Luke.

Brett Shut up with that.

Luke Fancy a dance?

Brett Na.

Luke (*putting both arms around Brett's waist*) Go on, dance with me.

Brett What you doing? Get off me.

Luke No, listen, please, just listen, right. Don't go off on one.

Brett Me? I'm going nowhere.

Luke You remember when we was in –

Brett Not again. You always get pissed and thank me but that bloke in Feltham had it coming.

Luke Not that. D'you remember that guy came and told us what could happen if you was doing graffiti on the trains and stood on the electric rail?

Brett (*starting to get undressed*) What you going on about that for? Tagging's for kids.

Luke Remember him saying that first of all your blood heats up and then starts to boil and then you dance 'cos you're so hot inside and you dance and you dance and dance and then your body explodes and because it's mostly water it spatters all over the place.

Brett Oh him. That plonker. The younger kids then went straight out and threw a cat on the line just to see what could happen.

Luke That's how I feel.

Brett What?

Luke About you.

Brett What? What have I ever done to you?

Luke No. I mean like a feeling of fire inside. Like what it must be like the second before it boils. Like someone

72

injected heated-up mercury into my heart and it's tumbling and spilling and pumping all around so even my toes throb and the roots of my hair feel like they're about to be struck by lightning. And the tips of my fingers feel so tender that I know they could feel the scars on your back even through your clothes and make them melt and heal. And I feel so ecstatic I could dance until I touch the sky. I don't even have to look at you. You don't even have to be here. When I think of you, inside it feels like I'm filled up, glowing hot and dancing. (*Tries to kiss Brett.*)

Brett (*violently pushing him away*) This is just drink, drink's making you like this.

Luke No, this is me.

Brett Get off. You get so drunk I've seen you kiss the shit off the bog.

Luke I would. I'd do that for you. If you wanted.

Brett Just shut up. Stop it.

Luke You take my name, who I am, but you don't want me.

Brett No I don't.

Luke But you'll do it with strangers. Why not me? You don't have to do anything you don't want. I'll do it to you if you like. What would you like? Or you can do – you know – anything you want – to me.

Brett I wouldn't do that to you.

Luke Why not?

Brett Because you're my mate. (*Pushes him away. Takes a can of lager from his pocket and holds it out.*) Here, have a shotgun.

Luke I don't want a –

Brett Have it. I want Mel, that's who I want.

Luke She's not here. (*Drinks the lager shotgun fashion.*)

Brett But that's who I want.

Luke Yeah.

Brett Come on, we've got to go out and find her. (*He makes a grab for his trousers which are on the floor.*)

Luke You'll be more up for it in the morning. First thing. Know what I'm saying. (*He crashes out.*)

Brett But get this straight for her. Not for you.

Luke Yeah. (*But he sinks to the floor.*)

Brett Tomorrow. (*He crashes out.*)

Gradually the room becomes light as dawn breaks to reveal Grace, Rose and Adele, all dressed in outdoor clothes and wearing rubber gloves. Grace goes to the window and opens it wide while Rose, holding a bottle of whisky, tips as much of it as she can into Luke's mouth. Grace then nods to Adele, who nods and holds out her hand. Grace cuts the palm with the knife. She then smears the piece of turkey neck in it and Adele then goes over to the sleeping Brett and drips blood on the front of his pants. Rose goes up to Brett.

Rose Brett, it's me, Mel.

Brett Mel?

Rose Have you got room for me in there?

Brett (*eyes still closed, opening his arms*) At last –

Rose punches him as hard as she can in the balls. He opens his mouth and Grace pops the turkey neck

74

into his mouth. Brett sits up in agony. Grace, still holding the knife, stands in front of the door to the outside and Rose and Adele in front of the door leading to another room. Brett looks at the blood on his underpants, then spits out what he believes to be his penis out of his mouth. He tries to go to the door, accidentally treads on the remote control for the CD player. Music booms out. He sees Rose, and turns. He realises all the exits are barred. Grace advances with the knife and he runs for the window and jumps.

Adele I thought you said no real harm was going to come to him.

Grace picks up the remote control and tries to switch off the music, but only succeeds in turning it down.

Grace How was I to know he'd jump out of the window three storeys up?

Adele Why did you open it, then?

Rose (*going to the window*) We were worried that you might go mental with the mace again. (*Looks out and then back at them.*) He's still twitching. We need to stay calm but make sure we've vamoosed before the ambulance arrives because, believe me, even round here they do dial 999. Firstly check the light bulb.

Adele I'm not doing anything any more . . . I can't . . .

Grace You will do as I say.

But Adele has gone. About the music:

What the . . . ?

Rose (*trying to get on a chair to put the light bulb back*) We don't have time. Let her go. (*She doesn't then attempt the chair but instead takes the light bulb and throws it away and picks up the piece of turkey neck.*)

Grace How are you going to dispose of that?

Rose We haven't got anything in for Melissa for breakfast.

Grace That?

Rose Might make a nice warming soup.

Grace For breakfast? Rather her than me.

The sound of ambulance sirens. They move towards the door. Grace puts the knife and the remote control in Luke's hand and they leave.

SCENE SEVENTEEN

Hospital. No bleeps. Adele has been dozing. She rouses herself.

Adele And, dear Lord, that is everything. (*then*) Please, please make it all come right. What's the matter, isn't that enough for absolution? Forgive me, but that's how I thought it worked. I've been totally honest with my own heart but I don't feel anything like the promised ecstasy. I still feel empty and awful. (*then*) Okay – it's not totally everything in my whole life. I know I've done other things, but I was young and they have nothing to do with this. (*then*) Fine, okay, I will tell if I have to. I know I did rather roger my way through the war. It was so exciting then, sex. People didn't really take it into their heads to be puritanical until the 'fifties. Of course I know it all counted as fornication and as such was not on. But as long as one didn't brag about it and was careful, oh so careful. They don't know they're born these days – feather-light latex and the like. We had to put up with things that looked and felt like that long piece of rubber tubing you get which comes on the end

of a cricket bat. Right how's-your-father palaver that
was. But now I see, God, I was just trying to satisfy my
hedonistic urges. Please forgive me all my sins. Please
hear my prayer.

(*to the bed*) Please give me some sign of absolution.
I'm so sorry, so very sorry.

Suddenly Brett sits up and grabs her hand.

Brett (*grinning*) You fucking will be. You're going to pay
for this you disgusting, boring old bat.

SCENE EIGHTEEN

*Rose's living room. The radio is on ('The Daily Service'
on Radio Four, long wave). Grace waltzes round the
room in time to the hymn, 'Morning has Broken'.
Melissa is still blindfolded and tied to a chair.*

Rose *J'aurais pu faire n'importe quoi. N'importe quoi.
Je me sens vivre après avoir été sans vie pendant un demi
siècle.*

Grace *Nous l'avons fait. J'avais bien dit. Nous pouvons
tous les avoir.*

Melissa What are you speaking like that for?

They ignore her and continue dancing.

Have you finally cracked up or what?

They continue ignoring her.

Take me blindfold off at least, would you please?

*They continue dancing and humming along to the
hymn.*

Grace (*as she waltzes past Melissa*) We'll decide what we
do and when.

Melissa It went alright then, did it? It did. I can tell. It's given you a right buzz, hasn't it?

Grace We did our duty, that's all. Enjoyment didn't come into it.

Melissa You said you'd let me go.

Grace We have to de-brief you first.

Melissa You gave your word. It's your duty to keep it.

Rose She's right.

Melissa Thank you.

Rose (*to Grace*) I did get a buzz out of it.

Grace Seems as though you've picked up more than your fair share of that awful street jargon.

Melissa You going to untie me, then?

Grace (*to Melissa*) When we feel like it.

Rose I'm not proud of myself, of what we've done.

Knock at the front door. Rose goes to answer it.

Coming.

Grace (*to Rose*) Don't talk rot. It's worked wonders. Look at you. No longer hesitant to open your own front door.

The knocking becomes more persistent.

Man (*voice off*) Open this door, please. Open up, it's the police.

Rose recoils from the door.

SCENE NINETEEN

The canal. Brett and Luke wearing wellies and overalls walk side by side pulling up rubbish and throwing it in sacks. There is a radio playing on the bank. Adele, with her own sack, comes towards them.

Adele Keep up Group A, otherwise we'll all be here all night. Where is Group B?

Luke and Brett look at each other and her and shrug.

Adele I asked you a question.

Luke We don't know.

Brett Marm.

Luke Marm.

Melissa, followed by Grace, who is gathering her rubbish with the aid of a three-pronged fork, and Rose come in behind them.

Adele And where do you think you've been?

Rose (*to Grace about Adele*) Look on your work, Doctor Frankenstein, and despair.

Grace (*to Grace*) You always were one for exaggeration. (*to Adele, but forced*) We're right behind you Adele, dear.

Adele But surely I don't have to remind you that this is community service, not a Sunday school outing. We have to have cleared the whole area up to Cassio Bridge Lock by dusk or they'll extend all our sentences.

Rose (*to Grace*) Just stop denying it. Thanks to you Adele's turned into Adolf.

The song 'Stuck in the Middle with You' comes on the radio. Luke and Brett look at each other and start to dance and sing along: 'Clowns to the left of us, jokers to the right. Here I am stuck in the middle with you.' Grace prods Brett in the bum with her fork.

Rose Leave them alone, Grace.

Brett You listen to your friend, old lady. I could have you. I could have you done for assault.

Grace (*laughs*) You want to go through all that again?

Melissa (*to Brett*) That's a joke. Stuff that's been done to you and you're going to do her for prodding you up the arse with a fork.

Luke (*trying to distract them, starts dancing again and singing along to the song*) 'Jokers to the left of me, clowns to the right' . . . (*etc.*)

Melissa and Brett start dancing with him to music. Brett takes his fork and pretends to shoot a bird in the sky.

Melissa Don't do that. It's unlucky.

Adele It's only a magpie, it won't hurt you.

Grace They won't be told, Adele.

Adele It's not your place to tell them Grace. Our probation officer said the Court told him that I was to be in charge because I was the most responsible.

Rose Because you were a big blabbermouth.

Brett And grassed us all.

Grace The one time when your line-shooting would have been the most honourable course of action. What do you do? Sit next to (*nods toward Brett*) his hospital bed and spill every truthful bean with a police constable sitting just outside the door.

Rose Thanks to you we've got two hundred hours of cleaning the canals.

Melissa Yeah, tell her.

Luke *and* **Brett** *(joining in)* Yeah, you tell her.

Grace *(rounds on Melissa, Luke and Brett)* You won't learn will you? You young people have no notion of respect, no discipline. It's all me, me, me. I want it now, now, now and I'll do it any old how. *(to Melissa)* Come here. *(She grabs Melissa and holds her.)*

Melissa Leave me alone.

Grace I'm not going to hurt you.

Melissa What you doing?

Grace Teaching you to do something properly.

Melissa What?

Grace Just do as I say.

She teaches Melissa to waltz.

Side together, side together. Step, one two three . . . *(etc, etc.)*

Luke I've always wanted to do that.

Rose I'll show you.

Pause, then Rose and Luke start to waltz while Brett and Adele look on open mouthed as Grace whirls Melissa around.

Grace *(to Adele)* Don't just stand there catching flies. Give your toy boy there some instruction.

Brett winces, but he and Adele dance.

Melissa We make a good team.

Grace Don't look at your feet.

Melissa I mean it. You and me, Grace. Together we could get up to some major scams.

Rose (*over her shoulder*) Don't even think about it.

Grace (*to Rose*) Since when did I take orders from you?

The End.